THE LAWLESS COAST

Smuggling, Anarchy and Murder
in North Norfolk in the 1780s

Neil Holmes

is a professional landscape and garden photographer, and has illustrated countless British travel books, as well as garden books and magazines worldwide. He was educated at Soham Grammar School in Cambridgeshire, and the University of Leicester, where he gained an Honours Degree in History in the 1960s. He moved permanently to Norfolk in 1990.

The Lawless Coast

Smuggling, Anarchy and Murder in North Norfolk in the 1780s

NEIL HOLMES

Larks Press

Published by the Larks Press
Ordnance Farmhouse,
Guist Bottom, Dereham, NR20 5PF
Larks.Press@btinternet.com
Website: www.booksatlarkspress.co.uk

Printed by the Lanceni Press, Fakenham, Norfolk, July 2008,
Reprinted November 2008

Reprinted November 2009, July 2011
by Newprint and Design Ltd, Fakenham, Norfolk

British Library Cataloguing-in-Publication Data
A catalogue record for this book is available
from the British Library

Picture Credits

Thanks are due to the following for permission to reproduce illustrations:

King's Lynn Museums – pp. 3, 15, 90, 136-7 (redrawn by the author), 142-3
Standard Chandlery, Wells – p. 17 (photographed by the author)
National Army Museum – pp. 19, 30 (photographed by the author)
Dover Publications – pp. 25 (both), 81 (bottom), from *1800 Woodcuts by Thomas Bewick*
Dover Publications – p. 112 (both), from *Rustic Vignettes for Artists and Craftsmen by W.H.Pyne*
National Maritime Museum – Front cover and Pages 35, 37, 54
Andrew Macnair – pp. 44, 83, and the fold-out map from his digital version of *Faden's Map of Norfolk*
Norwich Castle Museum – p. 81 (top)
Revenue and Customs Museum, Liverpool, engravings by William Heath – pp. 96, 106
Norfolk Record Office – pp. 118-9 (redrawn by the author)
True's Yard Museum, King's Lynn – p. 139 (photo by the author)
The Regimental Museum, Norwich – p. 145 (both)
Terry Greenacre – p. 77
Photographs by the author – p. 56

AUTHOR'S PREFACE

'The Lawless Coast' is a detailed account of smuggling on the North Norfolk coast in the 1780s, a period which witnessed illegal running of contraband goods on Norfolk's beaches on an unprecedented scale. With the widespread smuggling activity there came, inevitably, confrontation, violence and even murder, as Government forces tried desperately to confront the smugglers and to control their activities.

All the accounts which follow are true stories, and all the individuals portrayed are real people. Much of my information was acquired as the result of copious research at the Public Records Office, the British Library and the Norfolk Records Office, and entailed many months of painstaking sifting through primary source material. In addition, I was fortunate to gain access to original and informative manuscripts held in a private collection. My primary sources are listed under 'Primary Sources' at the end of the book.

I have begun the narrative with 'The Old Hunstanton Murders', which in many ways is a classic smuggling tale of the period, as it involves all the various departments involved in the war against smuggling, such as the Customs, Excise, Army, Navy and Judiciary, in addition to the smuggling barons and their retainers on the beaches and in the coastal villages. This enabled me to include explanatory boxes detailing the deployment of each of these groups, at appropriate places, to assist the reader's understanding of the events described. It is for this reason that the book begins with 'The Old Hunstanton Murders', covering the years 1784 to 1786, then follows with a 'Tale of Two Enemies' and other accounts from earlier in the decade.

I am grateful to Terry Greenacre of Clenchwarton for allowing me access to his collection of original documents, and to Dr Andrew Macnair of Foulsham for permission to use his digitally redrawn version of Faden's 1797 Map of Norfolk. This map, located at the end of the book, will assist the reader to follow the various routes taken in the detailed account of 'The Old Hunstanton Murders'. I am also grateful to Bernard Phillips of Wells for reading my original draft, and to Geoffrey Needham of Holme and Ken Walpole of North Walsham for setting in motion my searches. Finally, I would like to thank my publisher, Susan Yaxley, for her sensitive editing of my final draft.

Neil Holmes

CONTENTS

ILLUSTRATIONS

MURDERS AT OLD HUNSTANTON

SEPTEMBER 1784

Gravestones in the peaceful churchyard of St Mary's, Old Hunstanton, testify to the violent deaths of two men in the early hours of the morning of 26th September, 1784. The victims were William Green of Snettisham, a Riding Officer in the employment of H.M. Board of Customs, and William Webb, a private cavalry soldier of the 15th Light Dragoon Regiment.

Three local smugglers, William Kemball, Andrew Gunton and Thomas Williams, were apprehended in the village and were subsequently charged with the murders.

The following pages describe the circumstances which led to the murders, the careers of the participants, and the extraordinary events subsequent to the arrests.

DUNKIRK, FRANCE,
22nd September 1784

The harbour at Dunkirk on the north coast of France was alive with activity on a pleasant late September morning. The quay-side was packed with sailing vessels rolling gently against the jetties. Out at sea, a flotilla of boats, a billowing mass of mast and sail, made its way into port. Sleek and lively cutters and luggers, varying in rig and size, but all with enormous sail area, carved white, foaming patterns on the surface of the blue-grey water. There was a noticeable absence of squat fishing vessels and screeching sea birds; the mariners were not landing catches of fish, nor mending nets on the quay-side. Instead a more dangerous, more lucrative business was the order of the day, because Dunkirk was the export centre of the smuggling trade and the boats in its harbour were smugglers' vessels.

The gentle bobbing and swaying motion of the boats contrasted sharply with the frenetic activity on the cobbled quay. Seemingly endless rows of wooden, half-anker[1] barrels of French brandy and Dutch geneva[2] lined the length of the harbour and mingled with wooden chests full of lace and silk, while large quantities of tea and tobacco in oil-skin bags were passed from hand to hand, from warehouses to gangplanks. A constant, cosmopolitan chatter filled the air, a curious mixture of maritime dialects from Normandy, Norfolk, Cornwall and Kent. Englishmen and Frenchmen worked harmoniously, side by side. There was no hostility, despite their respective nations being almost continually at war with each other. They were business partners, above all else, and the smuggling business was booming.

William Kemball was one of the many smuggling captains present on the quay-side that September morning, and was co-owner and sailing master of a two-masted lugger named *The Lively*. He was satisfied with the price he had negotiated with a French wholesaler for the present consignment of 400 gallons of brandy and Geneva, together with 2,000 lbs of tea. The cargo was now aboard his vessel and he planned to set sail for Norfolk just before sunset.

Kemball was a native of King's Lynn, a busy and significant town and port since medieval times. He was the eldest of four sons born into the family of a minor borough official, also named William Kemball, a sergeant-at-mace who, amongst other duties, officiated at the town's law-courts at the Guildhall. The young Kemball's upbringing was relatively comfortable, his education adequate. As a boy he developed a fascination for the sea-going vessels whose presence dominated the townscape into which he was born. His first experiences of the open sea were aboard a merchant vessel exporting corn to the European continent. The return journeys made a lasting impression upon the young mariner, who learned quickly the significance of the intoxicating cargo stored below the water-line in place of ballast. This first taste of intrigue, cunning, adventure and profit remained with him for life. The young convert to the smuggling trade quickly gained the respect of his fellow crew-members; by his early twenties, he was employed regularly as first mate and pilot aboard

[1] A half-anker barrel contained 4.17 imperial gallons.
[2] Geneva, a type of gin distilled from grain and flavoured with juniper berries, was a very popular drink in eighteenth century England. It was first introduced by William of Orange almost a century earlier and was produced in distilleries at Schiedam, Holland.

King's Lynn Guildhall Sessions, late 18th century.
Sessions personnel, led by mace bearers, leave the court house. William
Kemball senior, father of smuggler William Kemball, was employed as
one of the bearers. To the right, the Gaol House.

3

smuggling vessels importing illegal cargoes from Dunkirk and Flushing to the Lincolnshire and Norfolk coasts. By 1777, aged only 25, he owned his own vessel, in partnership with another Lynn smuggler, Thomas Franklyn.[1]

Kemball was typical of the fiercely independent breed of courageous and unscrupulous sea-faring Englishmen who made a good living in the smuggling trade. Quickly he assessed the economics of the business, recognising that vast profits were to be made by importing illegally otherwise highly-taxed commodities. He recognised also the availability and willingness of large numbers of impoverished, landless labourers living in Norfolk's coastal villages, whose valuable services on the landing beaches could be bought for little and whose support would be unfailing. Kemball's favourite landing places for his cargoes were the beaches in the vicinity of Old Hunstanton[2], Holme, Thornham and Titchwell, an area of coastline which had the dual advantage of being remote and at a significant distance from the Customs Houses and Excise Offices of King's Lynn and Wells. Kemball cultivated the loyalty of the inhabitants of these villages, the majority of whom lived frugally, existing in cold, damp, disease-ridden hovels.

They supported families who were always hungry, frequently under-nourished. Their wages were pitifully low, even when work was available on the land in the summer months; in winter, whole families struggled to survive. The smuggling captains like Kemball and his partner Franklyn provided a life-line to such communities by employing strong and willing men, young and old, to help land the illicit cargoes, to hide them in their villages, to prevent them being seized by government forces, and eventually to transport them inland. One night's work on the beaches for Kemball would earn a village man greater reward than a whole week's labour on the land in the employment of the landowner or his tenant farmers. Loyalty to Kemball from his own private village armies was assured.

1 Thomas Franklyn's contribution to Norfolk's smuggling history is described in a later chapter.
2 The term 'Old Hunstanton' is used throughout this narrative, to avoid confusion with its present day neighbour, although in 18th century Norfolk it was known simply as 'Hunstanton' or 'Hunston'. The modern town and holiday resort did not exist in the eighteenth century, and its site consisted of arable fields.

Up to the year 1784, the smuggling business had been kind to Kemball. Apart from one minor clash with the authorities, which resulted in his appearing at the King's Lynn Quarter Sessions for assaulting a Customs Officer on the quay-side in the town, to the embarrassment of his father and for which he was fined 6d., Kemball's progress had been smooth, rapid and profitable. Now, at the age of 32, he was part of a large and elite community of smugglers, mainly English, living as part-time residents in Dunkirk, where he rented an expensive house and lived in comfortable style.

The *Lively* set sail from Dunkirk at 7 o'clock in the evening; she glided easily through the harbour channel and soon was on the open sea; the bustling port was quickly out of sight. The lugger was purpose-built for the smuggling trade, with a smooth carvel-built hull and two masts carrying four-cornered sails bent to yards and laid fore and aft. A bowsprit carried a large jib-sail. The *Lively* had been expertly constructed to provide its smuggling owner with the vital commodity of great speed. This had been achieved; she was lively in name and performance, and was a match for any vessel that the English Custom's Board or the Royal Navy cared to place in her way. In addition, Kemball and most of his crew were expert sailors, brought up to the sea and the smuggling trade from an early age; their knowledge of the sand-banks, shoals and inlets of the Norfolk coast was second to none. On the open sea, close to shore, on the Norfolk beaches and in the villages, Kemball was the master.

THE NORTH SEA, OFF THE NORFOLK COAST
Friday 24 September, 1784

The *Lively* sailed briskly through the turbulent waters of the North Sea, taking care to avoid the dangerous, devouring Happisburgh Sands, the maritime graveyard of many unwary sailors through the centuries. A moderate southerly wind had blown intermittently since leaving Dunkirk forty-eight hours earlier and progress had been steady. The *Hunter* Customs cutter had been observed, in the distance, cruising off Winterton and deterring smuggling vessels from running goods ashore on that particular stretch of coastline. The Admiralty sloop *Speedy* was anchored in Yarmouth harbour, undergoing repairs; so far, it had been an uneventful passage.[1]

On board the *Lively*, Kemball had assembled a crew of twelve men and a boy. Andrew Gunton of King's Lynn, known in the coastal villages of North Norfolk as 'Old Andrew', was Kemball's second in command; like his master, Gunton had vast experience of the sea and possessed a detailed and practical knowledge of the Norfolk coast in particular. Thomas Williams, also of King's Lynn, was another experienced mariner. He had spent many years on merchant ships out of King's Lynn, before being over-powered and forced into service by a Press gang operating in the vicinity of the port's ale-houses. For the next seven years he was compelled to serve on the gun-decks of three of His Majesty's vessels in the War of American Independence (1775-1783), during which time he experienced a daily diet of danger, harsh discipline and substandard rations. When the War ended, Williams was discharged from the Royal Navy and for the subsequent year worked on various smuggling vessels out of Dunkirk, before joining Kemball and the *Lively* in the summer of 1784.

By late afternoon of 24th September, the *Lively* had arrived at a position to the north of the Burnham Flats, an extensive sand-bank off the north coast of Norfolk. There, Kemball gave the order to anchor until nightfall.

THORNHAM BEACH
Friday 24 September 1784

At ten o'clock at night, a gang of twenty men had assembled on the remote beach to the west of the new harbour channel at Thornham.[2] They waited patiently and silently; only the occasional whimper from their horses and the relentless breaking of the waves disturbed the calm of the night. The sky was overcast and a light drizzle was falling; the overall darkness presented the perfect conditions for receiving ashore a cargo of contraband. The men crouched on the sea-side of the sand-dunes, and awaited a signal from Kemball's approaching lugger.

---

[1] The roles played by Customs and Admiralty vessels in the war against smuggling are described in a Box Feature entitled 'Government Forces Afloat', p.38.

[2] See the fold-out map inside back cover, showing routes taken that night.

THE GOLDEN DECADE OF SMUGGLING

Smuggling on the coasts of England in the 1780s

The maritime villages, remote beaches and coastal creeks of England witnessed the most dramatic scenes of illegal activity and violent confrontation during the eighteenth century. There were frequent and bitter conflicts on a scale resembling civil war, with the maritime counties providing battle grounds for a perpetual struggle between the Government and its forces on one side, and ruthless gangs and private armies of smugglers on the other. By the 1780s the conflict had become an unequal one, as the smuggling gangs became larger, wealthier, more organised and better equipped with fire-arms and fast sailing vessels. Government forces were hugely out-numbered and almost completely over-run, to the extent that large areas of England's coasts were controlled by lawless bands of vicious guerrillas organised by ruthless smuggling barons.

Today, smuggling stories and traditions abound in every coastal town and village in the country, and with good reason. Smuggling was, quite simply, a national pastime; a desire to cheat the tax collector of either the Customs or the Excise Boards, or both, was prevalent in all classes of society. In addition, smuggling was immensely profitable for all those connected with it. In eighteenth century England, Income Tax did not exist; instead, the Government's income was derived largely from Customs duties, first introduced centuries earlier and levied at all major ports on many imported goods, notably brandy, gin, tobacco, wine, tea and silk. A more recent and even more hated tax, known as the Excise, was levied on a wide range of domestic and imported goods; in effect, the smugglers' favourite commodities, if imported legally, would cost the consumer up to four times the smugglers' asking price, on account of the combined Customs and Excise surcharges.

Thus the smugglers had an instant and ever ready market for their goods. Once safely and secretly landed, their merchandise was eagerly purchased by rich and poor alike, by the aristocracy, the gentry, the clergy and the labouring classes. Inevitably, the Government became greatly alarmed as smuggling activity reached epidemic proportions; after all, its income and therefore its ability to administer properly the country in its charge depended largely upon imported goods going through the legal channels and the appropriate revenue being collected. The outbreak of War against the colonies in America in 1776 had placed an extra financial burden upon a desperate Exchequer. If the Government were to 'make ends meet' financially, smuggling had to be, if not eradicated, then significantly reduced.

To achieve this aim, the Government was faced with two alternatives; either replace Customs duties and Excise levies with alternative methods of taxation, or confront the malaise of smuggling with force. It chose the latter option.

In charge of the landing operation was a shadowy character named Perry Smith who, like many successful smugglers, has left to posterity very few traces of his career. He was obviously an excellent organiser, who hired local men to unload contraband goods on the beaches and provided horses and carts to transport the goods to temporary hiding places in local villages. He also arranged the conveyance of the goods inland to large towns. Most importantly, he was Kemball's pay-master, who put cash into the grateful hands of those men enlisted in the local private army. At the moment, on Thornham beach, his main concern was to ensure that the coast was clear of unwelcome visitors, particularly Revenue[1] men and Dragoons.[2]

At about eleven o'clock, the long-awaited signal flashed from a point 400 yards from the beach. A narrow beam of blue light, cast from an oil lamp aboard Kemball's boat, reflected briefly in a broken line across the waves. Kemball was ready to put out his longboat and to land the first consignment. Within a few seconds, on the beach, Peter Bullard[3], a part-time smugglers' runner and horse-thief, replied with a signal from a flaming torch; the coast was clear and it was safe to land the goods.

The longboat, piled high with half-anker casks, drew swiftly through the small waves to the shore and was hauled on to the beach above the water-line. Anxious hands grabbed the casks, already roped together in pairs, and slung them over the shoulders of the tub-carriers. Large oil-skin bags of tea were loaded on the backs of the waiting horses. Within minutes, the first convoy of contraband was on the march, flanked by 'bat-men' wielding enormous wooden clubs, along a narrow bridle path, to its destination to a cellar beneath a Thornham farm-house, or any other suitable hiding place. Meanwhile, the empty rowing boat had returned to the *Lively* to re-load. It was at this point that Kemball decided suddenly to abandon any further landings. He had heard the sound of a pistol fired from near the village and assumed correctly that it was a warning from one of his look-outs that revenue officers were

---

[1] The roles played by Revenue men in the war against smuggling are described in the Box Feature entitled 'Customs Officers and Excise Officers', p.12.

[2] The roles played by Dragoons in the war against smuggling are described in the Box Feature entitled 'The Light Dragoon Regiments', p.27.

[3] Peter Bullard's career as a horse-thief was destined to be short-lived. He was hanged at Castle Hill, Norwich, on 6 August 1785, for stealing a brown mare at Ingoldsthorpe.

dangerously close. He weighed anchor, flashed a signal to the remaining party on the beach and sailed back to the Burnham Flats. He would return the following night, to another landing point further west, close to the village of Old Hunstanton.

SNETTISHAM VILLAGE
Saturday 25 September 1784

Christopher Stangroom walked across the yard at the rear of his house at the northern end of Snettisham village and entered a small enclosed paddock where his horse was grazing. Stangroom was an Excise Officer, a post he had held for twelve years. During that time he had served in various parts of the country and had been appointed to the Lynn Excise District in July 1782; he immediately took up residence in Snettisham. It was his duty to survey and patrol the coast between Lynn and Brancaster, and to obtain information regarding smuggling tactics and future landings of contraband. He was empowered to enlist support from detachments of Light Dragoon Regiments billeted in local inns and ale-houses, and could lead these troops on beach assaults and village raids against smuggling gangs. Stangroom's life was lonely, difficult and dangerous; like all conscientious preventive officers, he was hated by the local inhabitants engaged in the smuggling business, and in a maritime area this usually meant the entire population. Unlike many of his colleagues, who frequently accepted bribes from smugglers, Stangroom was both honest and diligent, qualities which added to his unpopularity. His refusal to turn a blind eye to smuggling activity, in return for either goods or cash, caused him to be physically obstructed and socially ostracised throughout the neighbourhood. Frequently, he was in danger of serious assault or even death; just a few months previously, he had been badly beaten in a violent affray with a large gang of smugglers in Thornham village.[1]

The previous night, while Kemball was attempting to land his cargo on Thornham beach, Stangroom had been patrolling the coastal villages east of Old Hunstanton with Francis Young, another Excise Officer

---

[1] Three Thornham men were subsequently arrested, imprisoned in Newgate Gaol and charged with assaulting an Excise Officer, a capital offence. The story of this incident is related in a later chapter.

based in Snettisham. Whilst riding together down the narrow lane leading to Thornham harbour, they had heard the sharp crack of gunshot at about midnight. Experience told them that it had been fired by a smugglers' look-out and that, in all probability, a smuggling run had taken place on the beach. They had ridden in the darkness, past the harbour, over the dunes and on to the sea-shore where they discovered, by the light of a lanthorn, countless prints, tracks and indentations in the sand to confirm their suspicions. Almost certainly, the smugglers would try again the following night to land their cargo; Stangroom, in the mood for confrontation, would be ready for them.

Stangroom walked across the paddock at the rear of his house, carrying a saddle in both arms; he slung it carefully across his horse's back. He tightened the leather girth, then checked the flints of his pistols and slotted them into pouches on either side of his saddle. The pockets of his long, belted coat bulged with lead musket balls. He mounted and rode a short distance to the stable-yard of the Rose and Crown alehouse, where an attendant ostler took hold of the reins as Stangroom dismounted. The Excise man lifted the latch of the front door and entered the gloomy interior of the hostelry. He ignored the mutterings and hostile glances of a dozen or so labourers seated around tables, strode across the pammented parlour floor and climbed a narrow staircase to the upper floor. He knocked on the door of one of the rooms, entered and found there Sergeant Thomas Paine, one of five soldiers of the 15th Regiment of Light Dragoons billeted in Snettisham. He explained to the cavalry sergeant that information had been received concerning a smuggling lugger which would attempt to land illegal goods later that night. He volunteered no details; he did not trust dragoons, especially those who whiled away many hours each day in village inns, in the company of suspected and known smugglers. Stangroom's instructions were brief and to the point. The sergeant and two private dragoons billeted at the Rose and Crown, together with a corporal and private at the Compasses, would gather by Snettisham church at nine o'clock that evening; Stangroom and Francis Young would join them there. The party of five dragoons should be well-armed, Stangroom warned, and fully prepared for action.

CUSTOMS OFFICERS and EXCISE OFFICERS

Their Roles in the War against Smuggling

In the front line of the war against smuggling were the Officers of the Board of Customs and the Board of Excise, two separate departments in the eighteenth century. The majority of England's Customs Officers were based at major ports and had the mainly routine task of searching all incoming vessels and levying appropriate Customs duties. There were four such ports in Norfolk, King's Lynn, Wells-next-the-Sea, Cley-with-Blakeney and Great Yarmouth; each had its own Customs House and full complement of port officials. Unfortunately, only a small percentage of importers went through the legal channels; the rest chose the extensive stretches of coastline between the ports to unload their cargoes. These vast areas of unguarded beaches and creeks were the responsibility of specialised port officials known as Customs Riding Officers. It was their job to patrol an allocation of coast-line in search of smuggling vessels and to seize contraband goods as they came ashore; it was an extremely dangerous task in a most hostile environment. Riding Officers were mounted on horseback and were armed with swords and pistols. King's Lynn had four Riding Officers; they lived amongst smuggling communities in the coastal villages, and their 'rides' were based at Terrington St Clement, Dersingham, Thornham and Brancaster. There were further Riding Officers attached to the other three Norfolk ports; these men were posted at Morston, Sheringham, Mundesley, Happisburgh, Winterton and

Caistor; each port also appointed a Riding Surveyor to co-ordinate the deployment of the officers under his command.

The living and working conditions of the Riding Officers were unenviable. They were detested by the entire communities in which they and their families lived and worked. The labouring classes were particularly hostile, because the presence of Riding Officers in their midst was a direct threat to the extra wages and financial perks provided by the smuggling business. Riding Officers were usually local men with military experience and a detailed knowledge of the area. Their local background served only to increase the hatred of local people, who regarded them as traitors and agents of Government and class oppression. In the execution of their duties, Riding Officers were out-numbered by the smuggling population to an impossible degree; they were subjected to constant verbal abuse, frequent physical assault and total social ostracism. Even worse, many were maimed, some were tortured, others were disfigured for life; on occasions, they were shot or beaten to death. For those that survived, or at least escaped serious injury, there was a credit side to their dangerous employment in that they were relatively well paid. In addition, their salaries were greatly boosted by receipts of prize-money from seizures of smuggled goods. Small fortunes might be made from large-scale operations. Unscrupulous Riding Officers also pocketed considerable sums from smuggling barons by agreeing to 'look the other way' whilst illegal landings took place on their territory. While there was little they could achieve, as individuals, against large gangs of smugglers, Riding Officers were empowered, at any time of day or night, to enlist the support of cavalry troops of the

Light Dragoon Regiments on coastal duty who were purposely billeted in local village inns, taverns and public houses. Brandishing deadly sabres whilst mounted on nimble and speedy horses, a Riding Officer's raiding party was a force much feared by even the largest and most ruthless smuggling gangs.

While Officers of Customs were based at sea-ports and coastal villages, their colleagues in the Excise were more widely spread. Excise Officers were responsible for collecting a tax which was levied on both imported and home-produced commodities; so their responsibilities were not confined to coastal areas. Nevertheless, the Excise Board maintained a force of its Officers in the ports and coastal regions equal in strength to that of the Customs Board. King's Lynn, Wells, Cley and Yarmouth each housed an Excise Office, as did most market towns throughout Norfolk. Some Excise officers had a working brief similar to that of the Riding Officers of Customs, and were similarly deployed in villages between the ports. Excise Officers possessed greater legal powers than Customs Officers, including the greatly resented right of search and entry into private houses. Such intrusion was regarded as a denial of man's most precious civil liberty, the right to preserve the sanctity of the home. Consequently, Excise Officers were afforded an even greater degree of contempt, hostility and violence from society in general, than their much abused colleagues in the Customs. However, a generous salary, with plentiful opportunities for lawful and unlawful cash supplements, were sufficient to induce recruits in adequate numbers to the Excise service on coastal duty, despite the social and physical hazards.

The Customs House, King's Lynn, designed by Henry Bell and
completed in 1683.
Every major port in England possessed a Customs House, which
employed numerous officials to collect import duties within its allocated
stretch of coastline, and to control illegal landings of contraband. King's
Lynn's territory contained many miles of remote beaches much
favoured by smugglers, from Terrington Marsh in the west to
Brancaster in the east.

WELLS-NEXT-THE SEA
Saturday 25 September, 1784

Thomas Mitchell, a tide-waiter in the Customs service at the port of Wells, moored his rowing boat at the east end of the quay. He was one of eight Customs officials at the port whose main duty was to search newly-arrived vessels and to prevent goods from being landed without payment of duties. He had just returned from rummaging below the decks of a Dutch shallop in the harbour when Robert Jeary, Customs Comptroller[1] at Wells, summoned him to the Customs House[2] on the east quayside. Information had been received, from an unspecified source, that a cargo of contraband goods had been smuggled ashore, the previous night, from a lugger at Thornham. A further consignment of significant quantity would be landed at the next high tide later that night, at around midnight, near Hunstanton. It is unlikely that the information would have been sent by Stangroom, in view of the niggling animosity and distrust that existed between Excise Officers and Officers of Customs. The two departments rarely joined forces on expeditions against smugglers. If Stangroom had wanted help from Wells, he would have sent word to the Excise office there. Almost certainly, the informant would have been a professional, possibly a member of Kemball's own smuggling gang, who made a good living from trading valuable information for hard cash.

At seven o'clock in the evening, at approximately the same time as Stangroom was organising the deployment of Dragoons at Snettisham, Thomas Mitchell walked the short distance from the Customs House at Wells to the Standard Inn[3] on the quayside. The gloomy lamp-light was just sufficient, despite clouds of thick and acrid tobacco smoke, to display groups of red-coated Dragoons mingling with English merchant

---

[1] The Customs Comptroller at each port was a high ranking Customs official, second in command to the Collector. He was directly responsible for making returns to the Board of Customs of duties collected.

[2] The eighteenth century Customs House can still be seen, set back off East Quay, complete with a resplendent cast-iron Royal Arms. It was mentioned by Samuel Pepys, and was sold into private ownership by HM Customs and Excise in 1927.

[3] The Standard or Royal Standard, as it was variously known, continued as an inn until the early years of the twentieth century, and is now a shop and chandlery.

The **Standard Inn**, Wells, a mid-19th century photograph. This was one of the many English inns and alehouses listed by the War Office in the 18th century as suitable for the compulsory billeting of officers and men of various Light Dragoon Regiments on home duty. In Wells, the Fleece and the Red Lion were also on the list, as was the Pitt Arms in Burnham Market.

The facility to stable and feed horses was an essential requirement of all chosen establishments.

sea-men wearing blue jackets. Dutch mariners, dressed strangely in baggy trousers and large, clumsy wooden shoes, sat around tables with local fishermen and towns-people. Quarrelling and drunkenness now would lead to violence by the end of the evening, an inevitable conclusion given the volatile mixture of the assembled company. Thomas Mitchell forced his way through the crowded bar parlour to the kitchens, where he asked the landlord, Philip Batchelor, to lead him to the Dragoon officers billeted at the inn.

Captain William Gray, Lieutenant Jeffrey Wheelock and Cornet Henry Ellison, all Officers of the 15th Regiment of Light Dragoons, were seated at a large oak table in a comfortable and private first-floor dining room, set aside for the Officers' personal use. They had dined well on boiled leg of mutton, two roasted ducks and baked rice pudding; now they drank cognac, supplied almost certainly by the smuggling trade they had come to Norfolk to help suppress. Mitchell sat down at the table at the Captain's bidding, outlined to the Officers the information he had just received, and formally requested that an Officer and a company of Dragoons should accompany him, together with other Customs personnel, to Hunstanton. As the expected opposition was known to be well armed, with pistols and cutlasses, and led by the ruthless William Kemball, it was imperative, explained Mitchell, that the military force should consist of as many men as could be spared.

Captain Gray[1] was willing to oblige; recent inactivity amongst his Dragoons had taken its toll upon disciplinary standards. In any case, it was preferable for his men to fight smugglers on a beach, in the course of duty, rather than to fight foreign sailors and local fishermen in a quayside, alehouse brawl. The Captain appointed Lieutenant Wheelock to lead an immediate assault. With him would ride seven Dragoons billeted at the Fleece and Red Lion in Wells; a further three Dragoons at the Pitt Arms in Burnham Market would be added to the raiding party on its way to Hunstanton.

---

1 William John Gray (1754-1807), appointed Cornet in the 2nd Royal Scots Dragoons (1770); Lieutenant (1776); Captain in the 15th Regiment of Light Dragoons (1779). Retired 1788. He succeeded his brother as 13th Baron Gray in 1786. He committed suicide at Kinfauns Castle, Perthshire, following a failed love-affair.

Officer, 15th Regiment of Light Dragoons, 1780

THE LINES OF BATTLE

Smugglers and the Preventive Service

Throughout the eighteenth century, the degree of smuggling activity around the English coastline rose and fell according to the levels of import duties levied by the Government. Soon after the outbreak of War against the American colonies in 1776, Customs duties, and those of the Excise, rose to extreme heights, even by 18th century standards, in order to pay for the cost of the conflict. Correspondingly, illicit importation reached unprecedented heights on beaches throughout the country, and especially on the southern and eastern coasts from Cornwall to Norfolk. The expectancy and realisation of enormous profits from smuggling by all those who engaged in it, together with the inducement of unlimited prize money for those who successfully opposed it, caused a complete breakdown of law and order, especially in maritime communities. It would be a mistake to imagine that the smuggling faction was fighting for justice against a repressive fiscal policy, or that the government forces were simply doing their duty in a cause they believed to be right. Instead, both factions were motivated entirely by financial greed. The popular and enduring image of jolly and affable smugglers out-manoeuvring slow-witted customs officers and dragoons is an absurd and unrealistic misinterpretation. In truth, the smuggling gangs were led by cruel, violent and unprincipled criminals, who were confronted by an opposition led by self-seeking, avaricious opportunists.

Similarly mistaken is the view that the lines of battle in the long running war against smuggling were drawn up between two clearly defined warring factions, with the smuggling barons, their crews and mobs of retainers in the coastal villages on one side, and the various government forces on the other. Government departments in particular were so divided amongst themselves that their separate contributions to the supposedly combined counter offensive against the smuggling problem were severely hindered. It was the Government's intention that its land-based forces should liaise with those at sea, and that information regarding smuggling strategy should pass freely between officers of the Customs, the Excise, the Army and the Navy. In practice, Customs Officers frequently withheld vital intelligence from their supposed counterparts in the Excise, in order to avoid dividing the profits of a successful seizure. Similar disputes occurred between captains of Customs cutters and captains of Navy warships; arguments over prize-money led to frequent and violent clashes between the supposed allies at sea. Army private soldiers complained, with justification, that the lion's share of any financial reward was pocketed by their officers; in turn, Army officers accused Customs officers of an unequal distribution of financial spoils, by the simple expedient of plying Army sergeants with liberal quantities of alcohol in local ale-houses, thereby reducing their mental capacity to negotiate an equitable settlement. Any joint expedition which resulted in a seizure of smuggled goods would lead, almost inevitably, to petty bickering, financial haggling and dishonest dealing, and ultimately to a breakdown of trust and even to reprisals. Not surprisingly, the Board of Customs complained that 'the consequences must be of great advantage and encouragement to the smugglers'.

Further problems confronted the Government in its efforts against the smuggling epidemic: its officials, particularly in the Customs and in the Excise, were not averse to accepting bribes. Substantial inducements offered by the smuggling captains, either in cash or goods, enabled many landings of smuggled cargoes to proceed unhindered. The situation was similar at sea, where the Captains of Revenue and Navy vessels could be bought for an agreed quantity of smuggled spirits. Equally alarming was the conduct of some sergeants and private dragoons billeted in coastal village inns; detached from their Regiments, they were open to influence from local smugglers and at times indulged in their own smuggling runs, as did some deck-hands and mariners aboard the Customs cutters.

There were no such problems amongst the smuggling gangs. Generally there was harmony between all levels of the business, from the importing barons at the top, and the distributors and runners at middle level, to the local village protection mobs at the bottom of the scale. There is little evidence to suggest that hostility or even rivalry existed between neighbouring gangs along the Norfolk coastline, although elsewhere in England, and particularly on the Devon and Cornwall coasts, the situation was somewhat less harmonious. In Norfolk, the smugglers formed a united front; together, they would make a profitable, albeit illegal, living; divided, they would be consigned to a life of honest endeavour and poverty. Most maritime villages could produce its entire, male, adult population from the labouring classes to confront

Government forces at the slightest provocation. Thornham hosted a particularly aggressive village community, as we shall see in later accounts. Primitively armed, with pitchforks, wooden clubs and the occasional unreliable fire-arm, village gangs nevertheless presented an intimidating sight to any Government force, by assembling mobs in excess of two hundred men of mean intent. Such lawless aggression constituted a serious threat to the ruling classes, whose privileged life-style would have been threatened had the smugglers been politically, rather than economically, motivated. So powerful was the perceived threat that, at the height of the War of American Independence in 1781, the question 'will Washington take America, or the Smugglers take England first?' was raised in Parliament.

It was during this War that the smugglers experienced unprecedented freedom because of the severe reduction of Government forces on home duty. Private armies effectively ruled the coasts of England; marching mobs and armed retainers conveyed contraband goods inland almost without resistance. Smugglers strutted openly in daylight, on the beaches, in coastal villages, in alehouses, along main highways and through inland towns, in total defiance of the law.

This alarming situation changed dramatically when, at the end of the War in 1783, the full complement of Navy warships and Dragoon regiments returned to home shores with instructions from a beleaguered Government to repress the lawless posturing of the smuggling gangs. For the remaining years of the decade, the beaches and coastal regions of England were to witness perpetual and, at times, extremely violent confrontation.

BURNHAM MARKET,
Saturday 25th September 1784

Corporal John Stevenson, Private William Webb and Private Thomas Gristwood were tending their horses in the stable yard behind the Pitt Arms[1] at Burnham Market. It was eight o'clock at night and a steady drizzle was falling. The three men demonstrated little enthusiasm for their task; the day had been spent, like most days, cleaning their weapons, grooming their horses and keeping their uniforms in good order. Private William Webb had enlisted in the 15th King's Regiment of Light Dragoons on 13th January 1777, when the Regiment was based at his home town of Colchester. He remembered well that fateful winter's day; the soldiers on parade had looked magnificent in their red coats, white breeches and black boots as they rode in column on splendid horses through the snow-covered streets. He had been greatly impressed, as an unemployed eighteen-year-old, by exaggerated promises from the recruiting sergeant, who had proffered such inducements as a large signing-on bounty, the opportunity to wear the uniform of a royal and famous Regiment, and, above all, the chance to serve King and Country on the battlefields of Europe and the World.

The opportunity had proved irresistible to young William Webb and his friends; their collective enthusiasm had been carefully nurtured by the Sergeant with generous quantities of beer, and in a mood of general enthusiasm, they had signed on for life. Disenchantment followed swiftly. The signing-on bounty was never received, but was spent on their behalf by sadistic Sergeants and Corporals during a two-day drinking binge in the town's ale-houses. The weekly pay of nearly ten shillings had seemed like a fortune; in reality, after deductions for food, billeting, repairs to uniform, medicines and horse-care, the net weekly total was rarely above one shilling. Quickly, the new recruits discovered that their colleagues in arms were not 'brave young men of good character and appearance', as proclaimed by the recruiting posters; some were criminals who had been released from prison on condition they enlisted; others had joined the

---

[1] The Pitt Arms was named after Thomas Pitt, 1st Lord Camelford. In 1809 the property was purchased at auction by Robert Sparke, a local farmer, who changed the hostelry's name to the Hoste Arms, after the local and influential Hoste family, one of whom, the Reverend Dixon Hoste, appears later in this narrative.

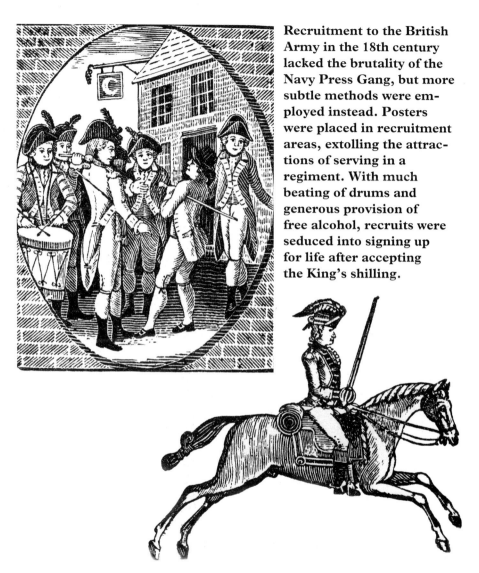

Recruitment to the British Army in the 18th century lacked the brutality of the Navy Press Gang, but more subtle methods were employed instead. Posters were placed in recruitment areas, extolling the attractions of serving in a regiment. With much beating of drums and generous provision of free alcohol, recruits were seduced into signing up for life after accepting the King's shilling.

A private soldier of the 15th King's Regiment of Light Dragoons, to which William Webb was recruited for life at the age of eighteen. The 15th Regiment was continually on Home Duty in various parts of England from 1777 to 1785, in a policing role, which involved constant confrontations with smuggling gangs.

Army as an alternative to transportation or execution. Mostly they were desperate characters, treated by their officers as the scum of the earth.

During seven years' service in the Dragoon Regiment, Private Webb had never seen action abroad. Instead, the Regiment had been continually posted to 'home duty', which meant maintaining law and order in England in the larger towns, suppressing food-riots and general civil disorder, and chasing highwaymen and smugglers in rural districts. Many months had been spent on 'smuggling duty', on the south and east coasts of England, an assignment both harassing and dangerous. Frequently he had been summoned from a make-shift bed of straw in tavern stables, in the middle of the night, by Customs or Excise Officers, and ordered to saddle his horse, to ride miles over rough tracks and in pitch darkness, and to chase an elusive and usually invisible enemy. Ever-present was the fear of ambush, of a musket ball in the back, fired in the darkness from behind hedge-rows. It was a kind of guerrilla warfare, hated by all professional soldiers at any time in history. In addition, the innkeepers upon whom Webb and his colleagues were compulsorily billeted were openly hostile to their unwanted guests, and always provided the cheapest and poorest quality food and lodgings. Local inhabitants, dependent in some way or another upon the smuggling trade, compounded the Dragoons' discomfort by displaying attitudes which were vindictive, obstructive and provocative in the extreme.

For William Webb and most of his conscripted colleagues, life in the Army was a depressing existence. Having enlisted for life, their only escape would be desertion or death. Some of his colleagues had absconded successfully, while others had been captured on the run and brought back to the Regiment to face horrendous physical punishment. Earlier in the year, the entire Regiment had been assembled at the Castle ditches in Norwich to witness the flogging of a captured deserter, who was stripped and tied to a triangular frame to receive eight hundred lashes. Such spectacles attracted a large civilian gathering, as reported in the *Norwich Mercury*. Another of Webb's colleagues had taken the ultimate course in order to free himself from the brutal Army life. He shot himself through the head whilst billeted at the Fleece Inn at Wells.[1]

---

[1] Joseph Hutton of the 10th Light Dragoons was more fortunate. For insubordination, he received 300 lashes at the Castle ditches, then was led naked through the streets of Norwich with a halter round his neck, and was 'drummed out' of the Regiment by being ceremoniously kicked on the buttocks by the Regiment's smallest drummer boy.

THE LIGHT DRAGOON REGIMENTS

The Army's role in the War against Smuggling

Eighteenth century England did not possess a centralised police force, or even regional constabularies. At parish level, problems of law and order were dealt with by elected constables, and at county level by County Militia and Yeoman Cavalry Regiments; all were backed by local Justices and Magistrates who had the power to commit suspected criminals to prison to await trial at Assize or Quarter Session Courts of Law. The system had worked with reasonable success for centuries, mainly because it was supported and enforced by a ferociously harsh penal code. Control of crime and disorder on a large scale, however, was beyond the capabilities of these mainly volunteer individuals and groups. Effective control was the responsibility of the Army, whose cavalry regiments, known as Dragoon Regiments, were billeted at major towns and cities throughout the country as peace-keeping forces. Their role was to control socially or politically motivated riots, organised smuggling and any large scale break-down of law and order. Regimental officers had to be mindful always of the War Office proviso that, whilst on home duty, 'the minimum necessary force should be exercised at all times'. (This was a precaution against the Army adopting the dictatorial stance which characterised its counterpart during Cromwell's Commonwealth a century earlier). As the Century progressed, the Dragoon Regiments became drawn increasingly into one particular area of almost perpetual conflict – the war against smuggling.

Each maritime county was assigned a Light Dragoon Regiment, to serve on coastal and other duties for usually a two year term. Each Regiment, consisting of 220 cavalry officers and men, having ridden into the county town or city impressively and splendidly in order to demonstrate its authority to the populace, would then be dispersed to strategically placed towns and villages around the county. The 15th Regiment of Light Dragoons, for example, rode into the City of Norwich in the autumn of 1783, to replace the departing 11th Regiment. Within a few days, the Regiment's six troops, each containing 37 officers and men, had been suitably deployed. Two troops were sent to King's Lynn; from there a party of ten Dragoons was detached to Snettisham. A third troop was billeted in the port of Wells-next-the-Sea, detaching small parties of five Dragoons to Burnham Market and Walsingham. The fourth troop of the Regiment was quartered at Holt, with detachments of three Dragoons to Blakeney and three more to Cley, while the fifth troop was sent to North Walsham, with detachments at Sheringham and Cromer. The sixth and final troop remained in Norwich, with detachments being posted to Winterton and Yarmouth.

These geographical postings were not adhered to rigidly; at the request of Customs Officers, Excise Officers or local magistrates, small military detachments or even a complete troop would be transferred to other towns or villages in the county, to be closer to potential or actual trouble-spots. On occasions, when specific areas of the county were being over-

run by smuggling gangs, Dragoons from outside the county would be brought in as re-inforcements. One such region was the north-west corner of Norfolk, a consistently lawless part of the coast throughout the 1780s and particularly so at the beginning of 1783. In January of that year, one whole troop belonging to the 20th Regiment of Light Dragoons, quartered at Bury St Edmunds in Suffolk, was drafted into Norfolk to assist the hard-pressed Dragoons of the incumbent 11th Regiment. As many as 40 Dragoons were imported across the county border and were concentrated within a small geographical area, on War Office instructions, in the villages of Thornham, Holme, Old Hunstanton, Heacham and Docking.

In the absence of military barracks at this time, billeting of Dragoons, whether in towns or villages, was imposed upon the owners of inns, taverns and public houses. The War Office had compiled an exhaustive list of suitable licensed premises, countrywide, which included the names of all establishments capable of accommodating officers, men and, in particular, horses. The system of billeting was compulsory; inn-keepers were forced to accommodate Dragoons and to stable their horses for a miserly 4d per day (to include food, small beer and hay). Even so, the War Office frequently refused to meet demands for payment submitted by the beleaguered inn-keepers, who in turn complained to their Members of Parliament of financial ruin brought about by subsidising unwanted guests.

A Light Dragoon, brandishing a deadly 37-inch curved sabre astride a
nimble light-weight horse. Officers of both the Customs and the Excise
relied heavily upon the presence of such dragoons when engaging
smugglers on beach and village raids.

Private Webb's reflections of despair were interrupted by the sound of a horse and rider at full gallop, approaching from the east. The horse was reined to a halt outside the Pitt Arms and Thomas Mitchell of the Customs in Wells dismounted and hurried towards the Dragoons in the stable yard. They were ordered to prepare themselves and their horses for action against a smuggling gang on a remote beach a few parishes distant. They were to be ready to depart within the hour, by which time they would be joined by the main raiding party from Wells. The Dragoons began their preparations immediately. First, an immaculate white saddle cloth, with yellow border and embroidered with the royal cipher, was placed on the back of each horse, followed by a leather saddle trimmed with fur. The soldiers themselves were extravagantly dressed; red coats, lined with white, with royal blue lapels from neck to waist, and royal blue cuffs. Their waistcoats and breeches were white, their knee-boots black, their leather helmets decorated with a plume and an enamelled badge bearing the legend 'Emsdorf', the scene of the Regiment's heroic victory in 1760 during the Seven Years War. All the men were equipped with a flint-lock carbine with 29-inch barrel, a bayonet, a sword with 37-inch blade and two pistols.

At nine o'clock at night, Lieutenant Jeffrey Wheelock's party from Wells, consisting of Sergeant Major John Leishman and six private Dragoons, arrived at the Pitt Arms. The crimson silk officer sash, worn under the Lieutenant's coat, glowed vividly in the light cast by lamps at the Inn. The three Dragoons from the Inn joined the column, as did Thomas Mitchell and Abel Dawson, the Customs Riding Officer from Brancaster. The whole party, now thirteen well-armed men mounted on fast light-weight horses, rode in single file through the village and past the parish church of Burnham Westgate. The soldiers pulled down the peaks of their helmets to protect their faces from the steady rainfall being carried on the west wind. Customs Officers Mitchell and Dawson advised the Lieutenant to avoid the coast road to Old Hunstanton, as this route contained the coastal villages of Burnham Deepdale, Brancaster, Titchwell and Thornham; all four villages were known to contain large numbers of active smugglers who would alert their colleagues at Old Hunstanton. Instead, the rough, inland track from Burnham Market to Ringstead was chosen. The column headed slowly westwards in the darkness, carefully avoiding large pot-holes in the parallel cart-tracks. The Customs Officers led the way; occasionally a

31

distant light from a farm-house oil-lamp flickered briefly through gaps in the hedge-rows. The column passed the tiny hamlet of Choseley; shortly, the party would join two more Customs Riding Officers at Thornham Ling Common.

THORNHAM LING COMMON,
Saturday 25th September, 1784

Samuel Rennett and William Green, Customs Riding Officers for Thornham and Snettisham respectively, were sheltering from the rain beneath a clump of trees at the northern corner of Thornham Ling Common. Rennett had been in the Customs' service since 1781; he was a local man, born in the village of Holme, and was both trusted and respected by the local population. He had acted as peacemaker during a violent affray at Thornham in 1783, when Excise Officer Stangroom was badly beaten by the villagers. It was strongly suspected that Rennett was in collusion with local smugglers; his relative popularity in the neighbourhood was unusual for a preventive officer and there may have been reasonable grounds for the suspicions[1]. William Green, a native of Snettisham, had been a Riding Officer for only a few months, having joined the Customs' service in April 1784. Previously, he had served in the 11th Regiment of Light Dragoons for a total of sixteen years and had attained the rank of Corporal before the Regiment was disbanded in 1783. He had been on coastal and smuggling duty for much of that time and was thus an ideal recruit to the Customs' service. A brave and resolute man, he was anxious to prove his worth to his new employers.

The two Customs officers left the shelter of the woods as the rainfall eased and the night sky began to clear. It was eleven o'clock and emerging moonlight gradually transfigured the landscape as visibility increased dramatically. From the east came the muffled sounds of horses' hooves pounding the muddy track, followed by the metallic rattling of sabres and bridles. Finally, ghostly silhouettes of the Dragoons appeared in the moonlit distance, as Lieutenant Wheelock's party approached the crossroads at Ling Common.

Samuel Rennett and William Green took over at the head of the column and led it due west, over Ringstead Common to Ringstead

---

[1] Rennett was eventually dismissed from the Customs service in 1789

village. Sergeant Major Leishman and two Dragoons were left behind at Thornham Ling Common, to watch and guard the routes leading to and from the neighbouring villages[1]. By Ringstead church, Lieutenant Wheelock ordered his Dragoons to halt and dismount. Only Mitchell and Green continued the journey to Old Hunstanton, in order to conduct a mission of espionage without alerting the look-outs in the village, or the crew on board the *Lively* as they came ashore. The purpose of the military operation was not to disperse the smugglers to another part of the coast, but to apprehend them in the act of illegally running contraband goods ashore. At the first sign of smuggling activity on the beach, Mitchell would return to Ringstead to enlist the support of the main party, consisting of the Lieutenant, Samuel Rennett, Abel Dawson and seven Dragoons. These men would remain by Ringstead church until their presence was required.

OLD HUNSTANTON CLIFFS,
Saturday 25th September 1784

Excise Officers Stangroom and Young had led their party of five Dragoons from Snettisham to the outskirts of Old Hunstanton village. The Dragoons were secreted in an enclosed field, close to the ruins of St Edmund's chapel, while Stangroom and Young took up a position on the edge of cliffs, about one hundred yards east of the Lighthouse[2].

With the help of bright moonlight, it was possible to see the village beach and local fishing boats resting on the sand above high water mark. The two Excise men lay motionless on the cliff-top, waiting and watching anxiously for signs of activity out at sea. At about midnight, at the peak of the tide, a beam of blue light was flashed from an anchored vessel two hundred yards or so from the shore. Stangroom sent his colleague along the cliff top to the ruined chapel, to bring up his party of waiting Dragoons. The moment to attack was approaching.[3]

---

[1] See Faden's Map. In 1784, six routes converged at this point, giving direct access to the villages of Thornham, Titchwell, Burnham Market, Docking, Sedgeford and Ringstead.
[2] The wooden lighthouse in 1784, with its enormous candle, stood on approximately the same site as the present day structure, which was built in 1830.
[3] For a full list of the names of the entire Customs, Excise and Army combined forces assembled in the Hunstanton area on the night of 25th/26th September, see Appendix B.

ABOARD THE *LIVELY*, BY BURNHAM FLATS
Midnight 25/26th September 1784

William Kemball and his crew aboard the *Lively* had spent the previous twenty-four hours hovering[1] six miles off the coast, close to the sand banks of Burnham Flats. All the mariners were by now anxious to unload their contraband cargo; their failure to complete the job at Thornham the previous night served only to add to the mounting tension. The crew did not relish the prospect of any further delay, as they were well aware of the risks surrounding their continued presence at sea, and of the danger of capture by either the Revenue service afloat or the Royal Navy, or both.[2] Kemball was dismayed by the bright conditions and visibility produced by the clear skies and moonlight, but he too was anxious to finish the business.

Furthermore, Kemball possessed the confidence of a man who, for many years, had smuggled goods ashore with great success and with little hindrance from the Preventive service either on land or at sea; he was prepared to risk the imperfect conditions. His resolve, and that of his crew, had been fortified by a high level of alcoholic intake, induced by many hours of tedious delay aboard the *Lively*. In a mood of optimism and high spirits, preparations to land the cargo began.

OLD HUNSTANTON BEACH
Sunday 26th September, 1784

At half past midnight, the *Lively* sailed towards the shore and anchored at a position approximately two hundred yards from high water mark off Old Hunstanton beach. One of the longboats was lowered over the side of the lugger, and four crewmen descended by rope ladder into the boat. Half-anker barrels of gin and brandy, roped together in pairs, were handed down from the *Lively* to the boat below, followed by oil-skin bags

---

[1] Hovering was a term used by smugglers and legislators to describe a contraband carrying vessel anchored off-shore, awaiting favourable conditions prior to landing its cargo. Numerous Hovering Acts were passed by Parliament, which declared the practice illegal. Like most anti-smuggling legislation, it was largely ignored by those whose activities the Government wished to curtail.

[2] The roles played by Customs Cutters and Royal Navy vessels in the war against smuggling are described in the box feature entitled 'Government Forces Afloat', p.38.

A smugglers' longboat, laden with contraband from a lugger offshore, approaches a landing beach in stormy seas.

each containing twenty-six pounds of Hyson and Congo tea. Two more of the crew lowered themselves into the boat, by now loaded to capacity with its contraband cargo. As soon as a 'coast clear' signal had been received from the landing party on the beach, the oarsmen set the boat in motion. The boat, low in the water, cut an uneasy channel through the waves and surf, but within a few minutes, reached the shore at a point to the east of the lane that led from village to beach.[1] The landing party, led as it was the previous night by Perry Smith and Peter Bullard, hauled the boat on to the sandy beach and began to unload the casks and bags at speed. Suddenly, a warning shot rang out, fired from a pistol by one of the look-outs. For a few seconds, all activity ceased and the smugglers on the beach froze to the spot in a state of apprehension. A second shot was fired, this time by Kemball aboard the *Lively*; it was his signal to abort the landing operation, and to return with all haste to the lugger. The landing party immediately pushed the longboat back into the sea, with only two oarsmen and the unloaded cargo aboard, leaving behind on the beach fourteen barrels of brandy and gin and twenty one bags of tea. It was imperative that the landing party removed the beached cargo with all speed, into the village, where the landlord of the Cutter[2] ale-house, Thomas Cooper, had agreed to provide a temporary hiding place for the goods in his cellars. The smugglers had scarcely begun to load their carts when they were interrupted by the ominous sounds of thundering horses' hooves and by the approach of a galloping cavalry force.

Christopher Stangroom and Francis Young had led their column of Dragoons along the cliff top, across the dunes and beach to the water's edge. They charged forward, towards the distant figures on the beach, with sabres drawn. The seven light-weight, nimble horses responded to the firm sand and spray, and galloped ahead excitedly and at full pace. The intimidating sight had immediate effect on the smugglers on the beach, who dispersed in panic, over the dunes and into the village,

---

[1] See detail of Faden's map on p.44, showing the layout of Old Hunstanton village in the eighteenth century. The approximate landing point would have been the area of beach to the east of the present day Clubhouse of Hunstanton golf course.

[2] In a comprehensive list of Norfolk's licensed premises dated 1789, there is mention of only one public house in Old Hunstanton, by the name of the Chequers, which was located opposite the present day Lodge Hotel. Evidence suggests that the Cutter was the same alehouse, which changed its name between 1784 and 1789.

The *Greyhound* Customs cutter, one of a fleet of 42 vessels built for the Customs Board in the 1780s to confront smuggling around the English coastline. Here the crew of the 16-gun cutter fire a warning shot across the bow of a fleeing smuggler. Note the lengthened bowsprit, a design feature which allowed increased sail area, which in turn produced greater sailing speed.

GOVERNMENT FORCES AFLOAT

Customs Cutters, Excise Cutters and Royal Navy Warships

*In the early years of the 18th century, Customs sloops and Excise smacks were deployed on smuggling duty, but not on an organised or co-ordinated basis. In Norfolk, the ports of King's Lynn, Wells, Blakeney-with-Cley, and Great Yarmouth provided harbour space for such vessels for limited periods, before they sailed away to other ports around the English coastline, on a rotation basis. The 1780s saw a great change in this erratic maritime preventive policy, and a new Customs fleet was commissioned. By 1784, the Board of Customs possessed a fleet of 42 Cutters stationed at major ports around the entire English coastline. The Customs Cutters of this period were truly magnificent sailing vessels; they possessed great strength, unprecedented speed and an intimidating battery of cannon. At full speed, with a vast area of billowing main sail, double top sails, wind filled jib sails and streaming pennants and flags, the Cutters appeared top-heavy; such was the emphasis on canvas and velocity. Each Cutter was allocated a stretch of coastline to patrol, over-lapping its neighbour's territory so that, in theory, complete coastal coverage could be achieved. Three of these new Cutters were employed off the Norfolk coast; the **Hunter** from*

Great Yarmouth, the **Experiment** from Boston and the **Swallow** from Hull, each with a complement of from ten to sixteen carriage guns. In addition, the twenty-eight gun **Repulse**, a beautiful but intimidating racing warship, patrolled the entire eastern seaboard, from St Abbs Head in the north, to the Thames Estuary in the south, on contract to the Customs Board.

As ever, the smuggling barons nationwide were unimpressed. With enormous profits and re-investment capital at their disposal, they responded by spending wisely on their own equally fast and effective sailing vessels. Some smuggling cutters were virtual replicas of those deployed by the Customs Board, which was not entirely surprising as they were usually constructed in the same shipyards and by the same shipbuilders as those commissioned by the opposition. There was the same emphasis on extensive rigging; also evident was the disproportionately lengthy running bowsprit to increase the size of the jib-sails, a refinement outlawed by Act of Parliament for all vessels other than those in the service of the Royal Navy or the Board of Customs. However, the smuggling sailing masters had little respect for government legislation and even less respect for the officers and crews aboard the Customs Cutters. Customs' employees afloat were regarded with the same degree of contempt and hatred as their counterparts on land. Their proficiency as mariners was not taken seriously by the masters and crews of smuggling vessels; they were taunted with accusations of preferring the safety of the harbour to the perils of the sea, of being reluctant to engage the opposition, and of being ever willing to *negotiate a peaceful and profitable deal without firing a shot in anger.*

The officers and men of the Royal Navy, the sole instrument of Governmental power genuinely feared by smugglers, were an entirely different proposition. Naval warships were usually commanded by energetic, ruthless and courageous captains, befitting the reputation of the world's greatest and most powerful navy. These men were also expert sea-farers, with great experience of warfare and tactical battles at sea against England's enemies, the French and Spanish in particular, throughout the world. The authority of an English naval captain, enforced at sea by terror and the harshest discipline, was legendary. Not surprisingly, smuggling vessels would always alter course whenever a naval warship came into view; if a willingness to engage and use its fire-power were not enough, then the presence aboard a naval vessel of a Press Gang, armed with warrants to forcibly impress recruits, would be sufficient to put the smugglers to flight beyond the horizon. The smuggling sea-captains were indeed fortunate that the Royal Navy's war against their illegal activities was restricted to the years of peace-time. Numerous wars in Europe and beyond during the eighteenth century necessitated frequent withdrawals of naval war-sloops from England's coasts. The War of American Independence from 1775 to 1783 had placed such a heavy demand upon the Navy that all vessels were removed from smuggling duty for the duration of the conflict. However, the end of the War in 1783 saw the return of the naval captains. Their prize money profits from the War had been negligible, and as a result they were most eager to rejoin the conflict with the smuggling barons and to prey upon the rich pickings to be had in English waters. Government land forces, as we have seen, were entitled to their share of prize-money from seizures of contraband. Naval officers were similarly entitled, but had the considerable advantage of being able to seize entire cargoes, together with the valuable sailing vessels in which they were carried. The resulting profits pocketed by the naval captains were enormous; not surprisingly, they set about their business against smugglers in home waters with great relish and enthusiasm.

*The Admiralty's newly returned fleet had an instant and beneficial impact on the Government's attempts to curb the smuggling epidemic nationwide, as warships were deployed around the entire English coastline. Four such vessels were ordered to patrol the Norfolk and Suffolk coasts in the Spring of 1783; direct from duty against the American colonists, the 14-gun brig-sloop **Speedy**, with a crew of 70 men, berthed at Great Yarmouth, while a similar vessel, **Brazen**, sailed into Kings Lynn. A larger warship, the **Myrmidon**, mounting 20 guns and 140 crew, cruised the entire length of the North Sea coastline, while another 14-gun brig-sloop, the **Otter,** was allocated the additional duty of protecting the herring fleet off the Norfolk coast.*

For the time being, until the next outbreak of large-scale war a decade later, the smuggling sea captains faced an uneasy passage.

leaving behind their horses, carts and contraband. A triumphant Stangroom seized the goods in the name of the King, his pleasure enhanced by the prospect of receiving a considerable sum in prize-money[1] for his efforts. His immediate concern, however, was to transport the goods away from the beach to safety before the smugglers could assemble a counter-attack. Accordingly, Stangroom commandeered the horses and carts, ordered his Dragoons to load them with the seizure of barrels and bags, and led the convoy along the beach, over the Common[2], up a narrow lane leading to the village[3], and into the yard of a farm-house belonging to William Clare[4].

OLD HUNSTANTON VILLAGE,
Sunday 26th September

While the Excise party of Stangroom, Young and five Dragoons were lodging their seizure safely at William Clare's farmhouse, further forces began to converge on Old Hunstanton village. From Ringstead came the Customs party of Rennett, Dawson, Lieutenant Wheelock and seven Dragoons. They had been summoned by Thomas Mitchell, but had arrived too late to assist the Excise raid on the beach; instead they experienced the embarrassment, on their arrival at Clare's farmhouse, of witnessing the unloading by Stangroom's Dragoons of several carts of seized contraband. The Customs Officers had been upstaged by their rivals in the Excise, and were anxious to make their own impact upon the village. With this objective in mind, it was agreed that the whole of the Customs party should ride to the beach, with Stangroom, in case of further attempted landings out of the lugger; it was a fateful decision.

---

[1] All illegal contraband, seized by Officers of Customs, Excise or the Army on land, or by Naval Officers at sea, was officially auctioned by Treasury agents. Half of the proceeds of auction went to the Treasury and the other half to those who effected the seizure. In the case of joint operations, the spoils were further sub-divided. The lion's share of the proceeds was always pocketed by the Officers, leaving the rank and file with a miserly pittance.
[2] The Common is now Hunstanton golf course
[3] The lane exists today, surrounded by modern housing, and is now called Smugglers Lane.
[4] Clare's farmhouse remains as the 17th-century part of Caley Hall Hotel.

A more desperate group of protagonists was approaching Old Hunstanton village from the north. William Kemball, whilst aboard the *Lively*, had received news of the seizure of his goods from his two crew-members on their return in the long-boat from the debacle on the beach. Although only a small part of his total cargo had been lost, an enraged and demented Kemball resolved to rescue his seized goods by force. Immediately, he issued his crew with pistols, muskets and carbines, already charged and loaded with gunpowder. Ironically, the carbines, which Kemball had purchased from an armourer's shop in Dunkirk, were identical to those used by the Light Dragoon Regiments, and bore the official War Office mark; in all probability, the weapons had been taken during a previous beach affray. Cutlasses and bayonets were also produced from the arms-chest on board, and Kemball, Gunton, Williams and five mariners descended into the longboat, leaving just the pilot and the cabin-boy aboard the lugger. Eight men in all, armed to the teeth, came ashore.

At about two o'clock in the morning, Kemball and his ragged colleagues, many the worse for drink, scrambled across the beach at the point where, some thirty minutes previously, the contraband goods had been seized. Perry Smith and Peter Bullard approached on horseback and informed Kemball that his goods had been taken to William Clare's farmhouse and were being guarded by two Excise men and five Dragoons. Bullard and Smith, it seems, had no knowledge of the re-inforcements who had lately arrived at the farmhouse, or that the total of opposition forces in the village now numbered twenty-one well-armed, well-disciplined men

Kemball led his crew over the sand-dunes and across enclosed fields, en route for Clare's farmhouse, to which he intended to lay siege. His confidence, already high on alcohol, was boosted further by the belief that a large number of sympathisers from the village, together with his own landing party who earlier had dispersed in disarray, would join him. His desperate army, almost overladen with weaponry, was a frightening spectacle to behold in the shadowy moonlight. Kemball came to a hedgerow adjoining the lane which led from farmhouse to sea-shore, and ordered his men to kneel, out of sight. He could hear the sounds, in the distance, of horses and riders approaching along the lane. He positioned his followers in a line, alongside the hedge dividing field and lane; each man presented his carbine or musket, awaiting the moment to open fire.

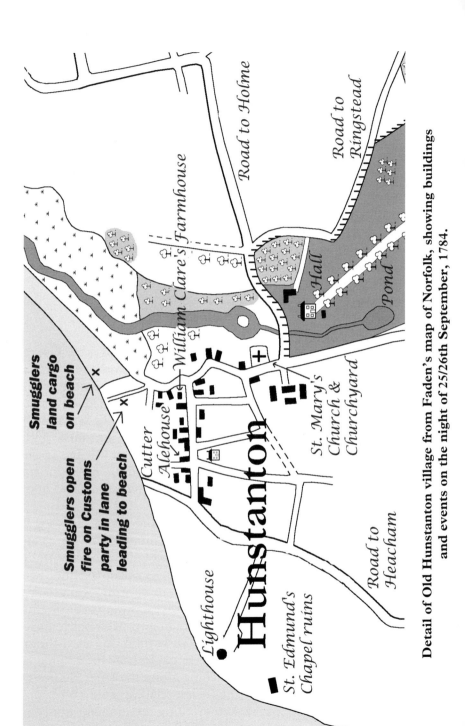

Detail of Old Hunstanton village from Faden's map of Norfolk, showing buildings and events on the night of 25/26th September, 1784.

A few minutes previously, William Green, at the head of a column of eleven Dragoons and Customs Officers, had ridden out of Clare's farmyard and down the lane leading to the beach. Stangroom also rode with the party, having taken the precaution of leaving Francis Young and the five Snettisham dragoons at the farmhouse to protect the seized contraband. The party rode past the gable end of Clare's large barn, on the left side of the lane. William Green was followed closely by Private Webb, Private Jardine, Thomas Mitchell and the rest of the riders, all of them clearly visible in the moonlight by the waiting smugglers ahead. Behind the hedge to the left of the lane, Kemball and his crew hooked their fingers around the triggers of their fire-arms; they took aim and fired mercilessly, at very close range, at a clearly lit enemy. Six shots, fired simultaneously, all hit their intended targets in one crippling and murderous volley. Horses reared and screamed in the lane and gunpowder smoke filled the hedgerow. Private Webb was the first to fall, as four balls of lead pierced his body, the first lodging in his skull, another tearing a hole through his neck, a third passing through his left arm, and the last ripping into his stomach above the navel. Poor William Webb, who had dreamed of military glory on the battle-fields of Europe and the World, lay dead in an English country lane, his body blown to pieces by the bullets of his own countrymen. William Green was next to fall, severely wounded by a ball in the chest; he clung desperately to his horse until the searing pain rendered him unconscious and he slumped from his saddle to the ground.

Confusion and terror engulfed the riders and horses in the lane, as further shots were fired from behind the hedgerow. Stangroom retrieved the situation by leading the way to a gate giving access to the field occupied by the smugglers. Having broken down the gate, the Dragoons, reinforced by their colleagues from the farmhouse, entered the field to give chase to their adversaries. Kemball, realising that he was heavily outnumbered, fled across the field towards the Cutter alehouse, leaving the rest of his supporters to disperse in all directions. Mitchell and Dawson, meanwhile, took care of their mortally wounded colleague, and conveyed him carefully to Clare's farmhouse, to which place the bloody corpse of William Webb was also removed.

Samuel Rennett became the third serious casualty of the night when, attempting to capture one of the fleeing smugglers in the field, he was shot in the thigh. Stangroom was luckier; he and a Dragoon cornered

Thomas Williams who was trying to evade capture by hiding in thick brambles in the hedgerow. Williams presented his musket at his pursuers and pulled the trigger; the fire-arm flashed in the pan but did not discharge its cartridge. Williams was handcuffed, taken to the farmhouse and placed under guard. Andrew Gunton was next to be captured, in the sand dunes on the beach at a place called Mason's Gap. Sergeant-major Leishman, entering the village after keeping watch at Thornham Ling, arrested Gunton, whom he recognised from previous smuggling encounters, for being in possession of a recently discharged musket. He too was confined in the farmhouse. Stangroom was delighted with the capture and detention of Gunton and Williams, but most of all, he wanted the elusive Kemball.

A party of Dragoons was despatched to the beach, to prevent any fugitives finding refuge aboard the *Lively* still anchored off-shore, while another remained at the farmhouse, to guard the two prisoners and the contraband. A surgeon from Burnham Market, Thomas Rand, arrived to dress the wounds of William Green and Samuel Rennett. The remaining Customs, Excise and Army Officers and Dragoons rode to the village centre and surrounded the Cutter alehouse. The Cutter was the only public house in Old Hunstanton village at this time; like most establishments of its kind in maritime villages, it was known to harbour smugglers and their sympathisers and was thus a likely starting point for the search for Kemball. Thomas Mitchell hammered with his fist on the front door, while Dragoons were positioned in the yard at the rear to prevent escape through the back door and windows. It took a full twenty minutes for the landlord, Thomas Cooper, to unbolt the door of his premises. During that time, there were sights and sounds of frenetic activity within, of people running about in panic, and of oil lamps being moved from room to room. As the front door opened, Lieutenants Wheelock and Polhill, Excise Officer Jarvis and a number of Dragoons, forced their way into the premises to conduct a thorough search. To their surprise, they found within the alehouse only the landlord, his wife and Perry Smith, who earlier that night had been directing the landing operation on the beach. Smith was discovered apparently sleeping in bed; he had removed his boots, but was otherwise fully dressed. In the absence of any visible evidence to connect him with the shootings, such as fire-arms or cartridges, he was allowed to go free.

Meanwhile, in the yard behind the alehouse, two smugglers were attempting desperately to conceal themselves in the tangled undergrowth of brambles, nettles and bushes. They had been inside the premises when the Dragoons first arrived, had descended into the cellar and had crawled through a low, narrow, vaulted chamber leading to the back yard. Both men now lay motionless as Privates Matthews and Stephens hacked and stabbed at the ground cover with their swords. As the Dragoons approached to within a few yards, one of the smugglers leapt to his feet, hurled a large brick at Stephens and fled, over the yard wall and into the fields beyond. Stephens fired his carbine, but missed the fleeing target as the man disappeared into the night. Matthews was joined by more Dragoons who approached carefully the spot from which the fugitive had appeared, their carbines and pistols cocked, their swords and bayonets at the ready. They came upon a deep hollow in the ground where they discovered a crouching figure, dressed in a sailor's jacket and trousers. He was dragged to his feet by his captors. The features of his face, illuminated by the glow of a lantern, were unmistakable. William Kemball was duly arrested.

WILLIAM CLARE'S FARMHOUSE, OLD HUNSTANTON
Sunday 26th September, 1784. Three o'clock in the morning

Kemball was marched along the main street, under heavy guard, to Clare's farmhouse, which had become the headquarters of a combined Customs/Excise/Army operation, and now served as a temporary prison, interrogation centre, hospital, barracks and, sadly, a mortuary. Outside, the house was guarded by a circle of fifteen Dragoons, ready to repel any attempts by smugglers and villagers to liberate Kemball and his two followers. Inside, regimental and departmental officers collected whatever material or spoken evidence they could gather. The evidence against Kemball was particularly damning; close to the spot where he had been arrested were found two recently discharged carbines and a collection of musket-balls. In addition, Christopher Stangroom testified that he had identified Kemball in the act of firing at the soldiers and Customs Officers in the lane. William Green, in extreme agony and close to death, declared that Kemball was the man who had shot him. Even more damning was the testimony of smuggler Thomas Williams, his crew-member. In an effort to save himself from the prospect of the gallows,

Williams declared that Kemball was personally responsible for inciting his followers to acts of violence, and that Kemball had ordered his men to open fire. He further alleged that Kemball had threatened to kill anyone who disobeyed his orders.

Inside the farmhouse, Kemball displayed little regret for causing the scenes of tragedy, pain and grief which surrounded him. On the cellar floor lay Private William Webb, his mangled body wrapped and covered in blood-soaked drapes. In a ground floor room, William Green, the Customs Officer, lay dying from horrific chest and stomach wounds, while nearby, Samuel Rennett suffered in extreme agony as the surgeon attempted to remove a lead ball from his upper thigh. Opium[1] was administered to both men; their continual groans were interrupted spasmodically by the hysterical screaming of Phoebe Green, who had been brought to the farmhouse from Snettisham to be at her husband's death-bed.

Kemball remained unmoved by the atmosphere of suffering pervading the farmhouse. While he admitted to being sorry about the fate of the young soldier, he denied all responsibility for his death, and portrayed no concern whatsoever for the injured and dying Customs men, or for the young woman soon to become a widow. On the contrary, he expressed the wish that all the Preventative Officers in the lane that night had been massacred. Kemball's bravado, clearly, was undiminished by his arrest, or by feelings of guilt, or indeed by the almost certain prospect of imprisonment and eventual execution.

WILLIAM CLARE'S FARMHOUSE, OLD HUNSTANTON
Sunday 26th September. Six o'clock in the morning

At dawn, the village of Old Hunstanton awoke to the sound of a solitary bell; its sombre tolling from the tower of the parish church of St Mary's announced the sad death of the Dragoon. If it was heard by William Green in the farmhouse, he must have known that, sooner or later, it would toll for him too. The surgeon could do no more for him and a

---

[1] Extremely primitive methods of alleviating pain were available to eighteenth century surgeons. Most commonly, drugs such as alcohol, hashish and opium derivatives were administered orally. In extreme cases, a patient would be rendered unconscious by a blow to the head, or, even more alarmingly, by strangulation.

visit from the Vicar reminded him that he was now in the hands of God alone. The same thoughts must have entered the mind of Samuel Rennett; his condition had deteriorated and there were doubts that he would survive.

A large crowd of villagers had gathered outside the farmhouse, to witness the comings and goings and the general activity. Messengers had been despatched to King's Lynn and to Wells to request military re-enforcements, and by seven o'clock in the morning, a further forty Dragoons had arrived. The authorities had captured a rare prize; three smugglers were under arrest, strongly implicated in the crimes of assault, and attempted and actual murder, to name just the more significant charges. Every precaution would now be taken to prevent their escape.

A further messenger was sent to the residence of a local Magistrate, the Reverend Dixon Hoste, at the Old Hall, Ingoldisthorpe[1]. It was a Magistrate's duty to commit alleged felons to prison to await trial, in cases where the available evidence was sufficient to warrant such action. Dixon Hoste was accordingly requested to prepare to receive and interview the three accused smugglers and to review the evidence of the witnesses in person.

HEACHAM, SNETTISHAM and INGOLDISTHORPE
Sunday 26th September 1784

At ten o'clock in the morning, Kemball, Gunton and Williams were led from the farmhouse and bundled into a high-sided hay wagon in the farm-yard. Each man was individually chained by the wrist and ankle to the floor on the wagon, while six Dragoons, armed with charged carbines, climbed in and sat alongside the prisoners. A team of horses pulled the vehicle through the farm-yard gates, past a throng of villagers, along the main street and on to the highway leading to Ingoldisthorpe. Every available Dragoon, Customs officer and Excise officer, numbering in excess of sixty men, was now engaged in the hazardous business of transporting the three captured smugglers through their own local territory. A party of Dragoons had ridden in advance of the convoy in the direction of Ingoldisthorpe, to patrol the open road and the poten-tially hostile inhabitants of the villages of Heacham and Snettisham,

---

[1] The Old Hall can still be seen today, to the west of the main road.

which lay en route. A further force of men rode immediately in front of and behind the wagon, to protect it from attack as it trundled slowly southwards.

The procession reached Heacham, where almost the entire population lined the main street to witness the rare spectacle. The presence of such a powerful military force discouraged any attempt to rescue the prisoners; instead, the villagers watched in silence as the procession passed peacefully. At Snettisham, the scene was repeated; potential hostility gave way to silent curiosity. By late morning, the column reached the gates of Ingoldisthorpe Old Hall. Kemball, Gunton and Williams were unchained from the wagon and were led, staggering uneasily in leg-irons and wrist-restraints, to a reception room inside the house.

Lieutenant Wheelock introduced himself to Magistrate Dixon Hoste and related in detail the events which had led to the capture of the three prisoners. Lieutenant Polhill, meanwhile, organised the defence of the Hall with the massive military force at his disposal. The Officers were well aware of the threat of counter-attack; large private armies of smugglers and their retainers had infested the North West Norfolk region in recent years. Gangs of up to two hundred men, equipped with fire-arms, cudgels, pitch-forks and anything else that came to hand, had confronted and often overpowered Government forces. Kemball was a popular local figure, whose arrest could easily incite similar large-scale disturbances. It was therefore imperative, from the military point of view, to complete the legal formalities with the Magistrate as quickly as possible, and then to remove the prisoners with all haste from the hostile area.

Inside the Hall, Dixon Hoste listened in turn to the evidence of Christopher Stangroom of the Excise, Thomas Mitchell of the Customs, Sergeant Major John Leishman, and Privates William Matthews and John Stephens; signed statements were obtained from each witness. Kemball and Gunton were then interrogated; neither man said anything incriminatory, and both denied any part in the shootings. Williams, however, repeated the allegations he had made at Clare's farmhouse in Old Hunstanton, and continued to blame Kemball in particular for the outrages. Accordingly, the Magistrate drew up a document which formally committed the three prisoners to the Norfolk County Gaol at Norwich Castle, where they would remain until their trials at the ensuing

50

County Assizes at Thetford the following year. The document read as follows:-

> 'William Kemball, Andrew Gunton and Thomas Williams, having this day been brought before me, Dixon Hoste, Clerk, one of His Majesty's Justices of the Peace, and charged on the oaths of several credible persons with having on the night of Saturday, between the hours of midnight and two o'clock, aided and assisted by several other persons at present unknown, wilfully, maliciously and feloniously shot at several Excise and Customs Officers and a party of His Majesty's 15th Regiment of Light Dragoons.......as they were peaceably and quietly riding along the King's highway in the parish of Hunstanton in search of (smuggled) goods, by means whereof William Webb, one of the said Dragoons, was shot through the neck and instantly died, and William Green, one of the said Customs Officers, was shot through the body and dangerously if not mortally wounded.'

Dixon Hoste signed the warrant for the detention of the prisoners and handed it to Lieutenant Wheelock. The manacled smugglers were led from the Hall to the driveway outside, where two horse-drawn post-chaises were waiting. Kemball and Gunton were jostled vigorously into one of the carriages and, once more, chained securely and uncomfortably to the floor. The carriage seats were occupied by armed Dragoons. Significantly, Williams was placed in a separate carriage; he was to be used, eventually, as a witness for the Crown, and it was therefore important to keep him away from Kemball's intimidating influence and presence. The post-chaises, each drawn by four horses, pulled away from the Hall at a brisk pace, preceded and pursued by the full complement of sixty Dragoons. The carriages bounced from side to side over the rough track way as they journeyed southwards over Dersingham Common and Sandringham Warren, through Castle Rising village, past the Norman Castle, and arrived at Gaywood cross-roads.

THE ROAD TO NORWICH
Sunday 26 September 1784

The Dragoon Officers had decided, wisely, to transport the prisoners to Norwich by taking the fastest and most direct inland route available, to minimise the risk of attack from the smuggling fraternity. At Gaywood, the column of cavalry and carriages reached the Lynn to Norwich 'Independent Cross-route'; it was an ancient road[1], well known to the Light Dragoon Regiments, and a route much used by coaching companies. Most importantly, the distance of forty miles from Gaywood to Norwich Castle was short enough to enable the potentially hazardous journey to be completed by dusk.

From Gaywood, the procession sped eastwards, over Gaywood and Bawsey Commons, past the ruins of Leziate Chapel, through Gayton village, across Massingham Heath, to the former market town of Litcham. Sturdy mile-posts were passed at regular intervals, together with innumerable church towers and post-mills which decorated the gentle, undulating landscape of central Norfolk. Local people watched curiously as two post-chaises, flanked by red-coated cavalry, passed through the villages of Mileham, Stanfield and Brisley. By Elmham Park, a large contingent of the 15th Light Dragoon Regiment from the City of Norwich relieved their colleagues for the last stage of the journey to the Castle Gaol, allowing the detachments from King's Lynn, Wells, Snettisham and Burnham Market to return to their quarters.

Lieutenant Wheelock continued to lead the escort column, through Billingford, over Bylaugh Heath, through the villages of Sparham and Morton, and over the Wensum River at Attlebridge. By seven o'clock in the evening, the Cathedral spire and church towers of Norwich came into view, and soon the hooves of sixty Dragoon horses echoed on the cobbled streets as the procession entered the City through St Martin's Gate. For Kemball and Gunton, the sounds of the City brought home to them the extreme desperation of their plight. They were now in truly hostile territory, which housed the headquarters of a Dragoon Regiment, one of whose men they had murdered so recklessly. Ahead lay the certainty of six months' incarceration on remand in a disease-ridden, barbaric gaol, before standing trial at the next County Assizes. While escape from the prison would be difficult, avoiding conviction and the obligatory sentence of death would, it seemed, be impossible.

Their journey ended, for the time being at least, when the carriages were hauled across the bridge above the Castle ditches, and came to a

---

[1] The present day B1145 road from Gaywood to Bawdeswell and the A1067 from Bawdeswell to Norwich follow the approximate course of this ancient route.

halt beside the prison's main entrance gate. Lieutenant Wheelock handed to the Gaol-keeper the appropriate detention orders, signed by Magistrate Dixon Hoste, and impressed upon him the importance of separating Thomas Williams from the rest of the prison inmates. Williams was a vital witness for the prosecution and his isolation was a necessary precaution against the near certainty of his being murdered, either by Kemball personally, or at his instigation, during the ensuing months. With this in mind, the Gaoler placed Williams in the horrifically dingy Lower Dungeon, in solitary confinement; the discomfort and sanitation were appalling, but his chances of survival were considerably enhanced by being separated from the other inmates. Kemball and Gunton were placed in the Long Ward, in the company of those who, like themselves, were awaiting trial, together with convicted criminals awaiting either execution, or transportation, or transfer to a term of hard labour on the prison hulks in the Thames Estuary[1]. The first impression they gained of their new surroundings in the County Gaol was the overwhelming stench from open cess-pits, and the wretched physical condition of their fellow-prisoners. It served as a poignant reminder to both men of the rigorous severity of the English penal code; for them, the future was as bleak as the cold, grim features of the fortress in which they were now entombed.

[1] Conditions in English prisons in the 1780s were exceptionally appalling. As a general rule, criminals and remand prisoners were not kept in small separate cells, but in larger areas of confinement or wards, where all inmates, male, female, and children alike, were thrown together. Norwich Castle had two such areas, known as the 'Long Ward' and the 'Stronghold'. The walls were plastered and whitewashed, the stone floors bare and devoid of furnishings, apart from liberal quantities of straw to provide basic respite from the worst depredations of the cold, damp and the inevitable effluent. Even worse was the over-crowding, which reached unprecedented heights and crisis levels in the 1780s because the American Colonies, having gained their independence from Britain in 1783, no longer imported a steady, annual flow of transported British criminals. With over-crowding came disease, usually in the form of rampant typhus. To relieve the problem, scores of redundant and rotting naval warships, minus their masts and rigging, were adapted as floating prisons. The Hulks, as they were known, were located mainly in the Thames Estuary and Portsmouth Harbour. Even hardened criminals shuddered at the prospect of being confined aboard these marine hell-holes.

Convicts being ferried to a floating prison hulk, anchored in the Thames estuary, from a late 18th century print. The hulls of decommissioned, rotting naval vessels were increasingly used as floating gaols in the 1780s, to relieve over-crowding in the regular prison system.

James Cliffen, the Yaxham murderer, spent two years of hard labour on such a vessel prior to his last criminal act, for which he was executed at the Castle ditches in Norwich.

OLD HUNSTANTON VILLAGE,
27th to 30th September 1784

During the afternoon of Monday 27th September, the mournful tolling of a church bell once again sounded over the village of Old Hunstanton. William Green had lingered in agony, on the brink of death, for thirty-six hours since receiving his mortal wounds; his beloved wife had scarcely left his bed-side during his brave but futile fight for life. Five young children wept and watched in disbelief as their father succumbed to death, cruelly cut down at the age of thirty-seven years. Phoebe Green took leave of her husband for the last time, determined to seek revenge upon his callous murderers and to provide for her fatherless children. She left Clare's farmhouse and took her family by horse and cart to Ringstead Yards Farm[1], where her father Daniel Frostwick was a tenant farmer.

The following day, the County Coroner, James Smyth, arrived from Dereham to conduct inquests into the deaths of William Webb and William Green. A gathering of 'good and lawful men from the County of Norfolk' was assembled at the Cutter alehouse to determine where, how and by what means the two men came to their deaths[2]. The Jurors arrived unanimously at their verdict that William Kemball and Thomas Williams 'not having the fear of God before their eyes, but moved and seduced by the instigation of the Devil.......feloniously, wilfully and with malice aforethought, did kill and murder, against the peace of our Lord the King, the said William Webb and William Green'. Andrew Gunton was not deemed to have been directly responsible for either death.

Two days later, the solemn rituals of burial were conducted in the churchyard of St Mary's, Old Hunstanton. William Green's coffin was lowered into a newly dug grave close by the south porch; his bereaved family, together with a large contingent of Officers of Customs and of Excise, soberly dressed in dark coats and carrying top hats, witnessed the last tragic moments as the 'honest Officer of Government', as his head-stone described him, was laid to rest. A few yards distant, another

---

[1] See Faden's Map. The farmhouse is now called Ringstead Downs Farm.

[2] The chosen men, mainly from the immediate Hunstanton area, were William Clare, Abraham Norman, Daniel Frostwick of Ringstead Yards Farm, Rice Stocking, Martin Sheldrake, Thomas Cooke, Robert Cooke, Michael Taylor, Jonathan Bloss, Robert Norman, James Houghton, Jeremiah Burgess and Robert Mason.

group of mourners, dressed in contrastingly bright red uniforms, stood in silent tribute beside the grave of William Webb. A poignant epitaph in memory of the departed Dragoon was newly-etched on his tomb-stone. It read:-

I am not dead, but sleepeth here
And when the trumpet sound, I will appear
Four balls Through me pearced there way
Hard it was. I'd no time to pray.
This stone that here you do see
My comrades erected for the sake of me.

The gravestones in Old Hunstanton churchyard of Private William Webb, who 'was shot from his horse by a party of smugglers' and of 'poor William Green, an Honest Officer of Government, who in the faithful discharge of his duty was inhumanly murder'd by a gang of smugglers in this parish'.
Webb's elaborate stone was probably financed by the Regimental Colonel and his officers.

EVENTS LEADING TO THE THETFORD ASSIZES
October 1784 to March 1785

During the five months' period from the capture and confinement of the Hunstanton murderers to their ensuing trials at the Lent Assizes at Thetford in March 1785, the legal department of the Board of Customs worked tirelessly, preparing the ground for a successful prosecution. It was a crucial time for both the Government and the Customs Board; control of the coasts and coastal villages of England had fallen almost totally into the hands of smuggling gangs and their retainers. Reports and letters from regional Customs Collectors, at all major ports, telling of outrages, assaults and murders by smugglers against beleaguered Customs officials and Riding Officers, arrived with frightening regularity at Customs Headquarters in London. Norfolk had become particularly chaotic and violent; only a few weeks previous to the Old Hunstanton murders, a crew member of the *Hunter* Customs Cutter had been shot dead off Bacton beach[1]. The Board of Customs had a duty to protect its employees; in order to fulfil this obligation, it was vital that those smugglers caught in the act of violence or murder should be punished with the full severity of the law.

The capture of Kemball, Gunton and Williams provided the Customs Board with a timely opportunity to set a terrifying example to the smuggling gangs of Norfolk and elsewhere. Judges and Magistrates, who administered the English legal system in the eighteenth century, were utterly ruthless when sentencing and ordering punishment to convicted criminals. There were nearly two hundred crimes on the statute book punishable by death, ranging from treason and murder to petty theft. Executions were always carried out in public in order to

---

[1] Robert Jay of Great Yarmouth, second mate of the *Hunter* Customs Cutter, was murdered on 10th August 1784, whilst attempting to board a smuggling lugger belonging to Charles Gee of Bacton, close to the shore of that village. Jay was killed by musket fire and was buried in Bacton churchyard. His head-stone, which can still be seen, makes no mention of the violent manner of his death, but instead records that he was 'unfortunately killed'. It is likely that Jay's family were unwilling to record for posterity the true version of events, for fear of reprisal from members of Gee's smuggling gang, which had a fearful reputation in the local area. Warrants for the arrest of Charles Gee to answer charges of murder were issued, but he evaded capture.

maximise their horror, and to discourage others from the ways of crime. Hanging was the most commonly practised form of execution; for notorious offenders, the 'launch into eternity' on the gallows was followed by gibbeting, whereby the corpse was taken to a prominent view-point close to the scene of the crime and suspended in chains on a gibbet. There it would be left to rot, and to serve as a gruesome warning to future potential criminals. Treason attracted the dreadful punishments of quartering for men, burning for women; brandings and public floggings were commonly inflicted upon both sexes. Transportation for periods of seven or fourteen years, or even life, to brutal penal colonies in various inhospitable parts of the globe was, in most cases, a fate worse than death. Certainly, the English penal code was savagely authoritarian; thus, if the Customs Board could secure guilty verdicts against the Old Hunstanton murderers, there would follow, without question, a carefully stage-managed display of bloody executions, calculated to send shivers of fear down the spines of other Norfolk smugglers.

Yet, strangely, one of the most common forms of serious criminal activity in eighteenth century England, namely physical attacks on Customs or Excise officials by smugglers, and terrorisation of whole communities by smuggling gangs, was the least punished, mainly because gaining convictions against smugglers was spectacularly difficult. Apart from ten members of the notorious Hawkhurst gang in Sussex, who were convicted and hanged as a result of murder trials at Chichester and the Old Bailey in 1749, there were very few executions of smugglers throughout the eighteenth century. There were numerous obstacles confronting those engaged in obtaining convictions against smugglers accused of serious assault or even murder. Smugglers who were tried in their own native counties frequently gained preference from juries which contained smugglers' sympathisers in sufficient numbers to influence the final verdict. Independent witnesses willing to testify against smugglers were difficult to find, because of the fear of inevitable and terrible revenge. Smuggling outrages occurred usually at night and involved many participants; it was difficult, therefore, to identify individual offenders. In addition, smuggling gangs were so well organised that the services of professional 'witnesses' were easily bought; they would appear for the defence to quote entirely spurious evidence and to contradict prosecution witnesses. Finally, the smuggling fraternity had, it seemed, unlimited funds with which to engage experienced defence lawyers, and to pay handsome cash sums to perjurers.

The Customs Board was well aware of the difficulties it faced, and worked energetically to overcome them. With support from the Privy Council, the Treasury Solicitor, the War Office and the Board of Excise, the legal department at Customs Headquarters in London conducted a widespread and determined campaign to ensure that Kemball and Gunton should end their days at the end of a rope. No financial expense was spared; Robert Whincop[1], an eminent solicitor practising in King's Lynn, was engaged to conduct operations on the Customs' behalf within the county of Norfolk. He arranged the serving of subpoenas on witnesses for the prosecution, and obtained their detailed, written statements. A total of twenty-two witnesses were subpoenaed to attend the future trials; of these, eleven were Officers and Privates in the 15th Regiment of Light Dragoons, and six were either Customs or Excise Officers. Significantly, only three civilians were prepared to give evidence. However, Whincop provided the Customs Board with a potential trump card in the form of the testimony of Thomas Williams, one of Kemball's accomplices arrested at Old Hunstanton. During a secret meeting in the prison at Norwich Castle, Whincop took from Williams a detailed and most damning indictment of his former smuggling colleagues; in return for 'turning King's evidence', Williams himself would be spared from prosecution. It was, perhaps, indicative of the Customs Board's lack of confidence in a positive outcome at the forthcoming trials that such a cynical deal was struck. In effect, the prosecuting authorities were offering a free pardon to a man who was clearly guilty as an accessory to murder, and who was motivated solely by a desire to save his own neck.

Whincop's next task was to investigate thoroughly the backgrounds and personalities of the men who would eventually deliver judgement upon Kemball and Gunton at the Thetford Assizes. As usual, a total of thirty-six jurors was empanelled to serve for the duration of the Lent

---

[1] A plaque on the façade of Whincop House, 29 Tower Street (formerly Baxters Row), King's Lynn, records that the Georgian town house was named after its resident Robert Whincop (1733-1803). In addition to being Lynn's prominent solicitor, he was also Deputy Collector of Customs and, from 1785 to 1803, the Town Clerk. His nephew, also Robert Whincop, succeeded his uncle as Town Clerk, and held the position from 1803 to 1837

Assizes; their names were selected from the Norfolk county voters' list[1]. Each juror was investigated thoroughly by Whincop and his staff, with particular attention being given to rumours and allegations of complicity with the smuggling trade. A surviving list of the names of all thirty-six jurors, compiled by Whincop, contains brief descriptions of his conclusions. Some jurors were found to be acceptable; their names were annotated with comments such as 'not suspected to have connections with smuggling', or 'an upright, fair dealing man', or 'averse to illicit practice'. Others were deemed to be entirely unacceptable. 'Closely connected with smuggling' was the description of William Hardy of Rockland All Saints; James Gooch of North Lopham was considered 'doubtful', and Thomas Syder of Banham as a 'suspected, doubtful person'. All three would be challenged eventually by the prosecution and debarred from sitting in judgement on the initial trial of Kemball and Gunton.[2]

By March 1785, the Customs Board had become increasingly apprehensive about the outcome of the trials. Letters despatched from Customs Headquarters in London to the Collector at King's Lynn made frequent reference to what should be done 'in the event of a not guilty verdict being delivered'. On the very eve of the Assizes, emergency plans were drawn up to counter such an eventuality. Whincop travelled again to Norwich Castle to take from Thomas Williams a further statement, relating to the illegal landing of smuggled goods on Old Hunstanton beach by Kemball and Gunton prior to the murders in the village. Writs authorising re-arrest were issued against the two prisoners 'in order to detain them in custody in case they are acquitted of murder', and to summon them to appear at an Exchequer trial at Westminster on a charge of smuggling (as opposed to murder) after the Assizes.

The Sheriff of Norfolk was also apprehensive. He was responsible ultimately for the safe custody of two of the nation's most notorious prisoners, within the seemingly impregnable walls of the County's largest and most secure prison. Despite this assurance, he contacted the War Office, in January 1785, expressing his fears of possible rescue attempts.

---

[1] The right to vote (and therefore the right to sit on a Jury) was restricted to a very small percentage of the male population in the eighteenth century. Only freeholders of property possessed these rights.

[2] The names and parishes of residence of all the empanelled jurors are listed in the Appendix A.

'The keeper of the County Gaol', he wrote, 'having now nearly forty persons in his custody, many of whom are of the most abandoned and desperate principles, and confined for murder, forgery and other atrocious crimes, has informed me that he has certain information of a determination to rescue them by a gang of smugglers.'

The threat was taken very seriously; Captain William Gray of the 15th Regiment of Light Dragoons was given the task of defending the Castle against possible attack. For two months, up to the time when the prisoners would leave the city to attend the Assizes at Thetford, the Castle Gaol was provided with a garrison of Dragoons to keep watch, day and night, for the threatened rescue attempt.

At the beginning of March 1785, as the commencement of the Lent Assizes drew near, the Sheriff wrote again to the War Office, expressing further fears for the security of his prisoners. On this occasion, the Sheriff claimed to have uncovered a plot to rescue Kemball and Gunton during the course of their journey from Norwich Castle to Thetford gaol.

'The felons who are to be conveyed are upwards of twenty in number', wrote the Sheriff, 'many of them of the most abandoned principles and desperate conduct, particularly Kemball, Gunton and Williams[1], notorious smugglers committed for wilful murder; many others of them are committed for burglary, highway robbery and other atrocious crimes'.

The Sheriff requested a large military force to accompany the prisoners in transit, because of

'well-founded apprehensions that a plan is laid for the rescue of the aforesaid murderers on their way to, or at, Thetford, by the numerous gangs of murderous smugglers which infest this county. This plan is the more readily to be carried into execution by reason of the distance from Norwich Castle to Thetford Gaol, which is upwards of thirty miles and the road lying thro' a thinly inhabited part of the county.'

In addition, the Sheriff was concerned that the gaol at Thetford was

---

[1] The Sheriff seemed to be unaware that Williams had 'turned King's evidence' and that he would be travelling to Thetford independently of the felons facing trial.

'not sufficiently strong for the security of so large a number of felons during the Assizes"[1]

The War Office, once again, was sympathetic to the request and immediately despatched a letter to the Officer commanding the 15th Regiment in Norwich.

'There are well-founded apprehensions', wrote the Secretary of State for War, 'of a plan being laid for the rescue of the felons now in Norwich gaol either on their way to, or at, Thetford, where they are to be tried, and that a military guard is absolutely necessary for the security of the said prisoners. It is His Majesty's pleasure that you cause such a detachment as shall be judged sufficient ....to be aiding and assisting the High Sheriff, his deputy and officers, and any of the civil Magistrates of Norfolk, upon their requisition, in safely escorting the said felons to Thetford Gaol, in guarding them while there, and in conveying them back to Norwich. It is His Majesty's further pleasure that the Detachment (of dragoons) hereby ordered shall continue on this duty ....until the persons charged with the murders be disposed of in due course of law.'

It remained to be seen which direction the 'due course of law' would take.

The Lent Assizes at Thetford, at which Kemball, Gunton and twenty-one other prisoners would be tried for various felonies, were scheduled to commence on 22nd March, 1785. At the well-guarded county gaol in Norwich Castle, preparations to transport the men and women to the Assizes were begun.

THE ROAD TO THETFORD,
16 March 1785

At 9 o'clock in the morning of 16 March 1785, two open-topped, horse-drawn carts drew up outside the main door of the County Gaol at Norwich Castle. From inside the Castle emerged twenty-three heavily guarded prisoners. They shuffled awkwardly in rigid leg-irons as they were led by turnkeys and dragoons to the waiting carts. It was a cold,

[1] Correspondence between the Sheriff of Norfolk and the War Office is contained in War Office documents at the Public Record Office.

grey, damp mid-March morning; the prisoners sat with shoulders hunched in a vain attempt to resist the chill in the air. As the carts were hauled over the bridge across the Castle ditches, and bounced and trundled over the cobbled streets of the city, onlookers assembled in large vociferous groups to witness the annual procession. The prisoners in each cart sat in two inward facing rows, their heads drooped, their gaze fixed to the floor, to avoid the attentions and insults of the jeering mob. The cavalry escort rode ahead to clear a way through the jostling crowds; alongside the carts were more dragoons, with sabres drawn, to protect the forlorn prisoners from the worst of the physical abuse. Garbage was hurled from the crowd, in the traditional manner, although most of the populace watched curiously to catch sight of, and identify, the infamous smugglers. The procession left the city through St Stephen's Gate to begin the twenty-eight mile journey, through mainly uninhabited countryside, to Thetford.

The Sheriff of Norfolk's request for a military force to accompany the felons to the Assizes was well heeded. Advance cavalry parties patrolled the road, the villages and market towns ahead, while an escort of dragoons rode in close attendance to the prison carts. For the previous six hundred years, ever since the twelfth century, the annual procession from Norwich to Thetford, carrying felons accused of serious offences[1] to the Lent Assizes, had followed much the same route as it did on this occasion, through the villages of Eaton, Cringleford and Hethersett, over the extensive Hethersett Common, to the market town of Wymondham. The first stage of the journey ended there, without incident, to the relief of Captain William Gray, the officer commanding the escort detachment of Dragoons.

Kemball and Gunton's reluctant companions, chained alongside them on the prison carts, were to be tried for an assortment of offences, most of which carried the penalty of death. Facing capital conviction were James Cliffen of Yaxham, for murder on the highway; Robert Randall, for highway robbery at Costessey; Joseph Buttisant, for stealing a sheep at North Walsham; Robert Cademy, for stealing twelve ewes at Tattersett; Thomas Lond and James Booty, for stealing hogs at Kirby Cane; William Newland, for forgery; John Clamp, for stealing two sheep

---

[1] Assizes were held twice yearly in all of the English counties. In Norfolk, the Lent Assizes were held at Thetford in March and the Summer Assizes at Norwich in July.

at Stanhoe; John Flint, for stealing a mare at Emneth; John Garner, for stealing five pigs at East Dereham; John Ferret, for house-breaking at Great Yarmouth, and Thomas Sparshall, of Beetley, for stealing an ass. All could expect conviction and execution, although for some there existed the hope of a merciful reprieve and the imposition of an alternative, commuted sentence of transportation for life to a penal colony abroad. There were nine other prisoners on the carts, mostly women, accused of burglary, theft and arson, for which alleged crimes they could expect little or no mercy from the Judge and Jury.

The procession of carts, prisoners and dragoons left Wymondham and travelled south westwards over Wymondham Causeway, Sutton Common and Attleborough Mere. The cold, damp drizzle turned to sleet and snow in a bitter northerly wind, bringing further physical discomfort to the wretched, hunched figures on the open carts.[1] Of all the prisoners, only Kemball and Gunton had reason for some degree of optimism, ironically in view of the extreme seriousness of their alleged crimes. Yet it remained to be seen whether or not the Jury at the forthcoming Assizes would find the two men guilty. In the maritime counties of England, there was widespread sympathy, even respect, for the smuggling fraternity and its illegal trafficking of commodities which were both desirable and affordable, being marketed free from the burden of hated taxation. In the minds of many eighteenth century jurors, it was a far worse crime to steal a man's horse than to take the life of an official engaged in the business of enforcing taxation. In addition, Kemball and Gunton, during their confinement at the County Gaol, had used their dubious contacts, together with their financial assets, to great advantage. Soon after their arrival at the prison, they had bribed the head turnkey, Thomas Cutting, into providing a relatively comfortable cell, apart from the other prisoners in the wards. They were allowed the privilege of receiving visitors in their separate cell, on which occasions the two smugglers were able to enlist witnesses to testify on their behalf at the forthcoming Assizes. Each enlisted witness was allocated a specific and,

---

[1] The prisoners had already suffered extreme deprivation during the severe winter of 1784/1785, and the conditions within the prison at Norwich Castle were exacerbated by intensely low temperatures. Parson Woodforde of the parish of Weston Longville, ten miles to the west of Norwich, kept a detailed Diary, in which he recorded that, on 28th February 1785, 'the frost severer than ever in the night as it even froze the Chamber Pots under the beds...Most bitter cold today indeed, and likely to continue....'

no doubt, entirely spurious version of the events which had occurred during the night of the murders in Old Hunstanton. Briefed by an experienced defence lawyer, engaged regardless of expense, the defence witnesses would provide credible alibis for both Kemball and Gunton; furthermore, additional witnesses would attempt to discredit the evidence to be given by the principal prosecution witness, Thomas Williams. Even the head turnkey would be called as a witness on behalf of the alleged murderers. Finally, the two smugglers would have been encouraged by the knowledge that a Norfolk Jury had acquitted one of their colleagues, Thomas Franklyn, at the Thetford Assizes in March 1783, despite overwhelming evidence that he had violently assaulted and maimed an Excise Officer in Thornham village.[1] Whilst some of their companions on the prison carts were resigned to the fate of execution, Kemball and Gunton could travel with hope; all was not yet lost.

The journey continued, through Attleborough, over Fettlebridge Common and across the remote heathlands of Larling, Bridgeham and Kilverstone. At about 3 o'clock in the afternoon, the procession entered the bustling market town of Thetford and came to a halt outside the squalid gaol-house. Townspeople lined the streets in great numbers to welcome the twenty-three prisoners who would provide popular entertainment over the coming days. At the Assizes, some would be sentenced to hang, some to be transported, others to be flogged or branded. There would be an abundance of onlookers around the Court-house to await news of the various punishments handed out to the unfortunate wretches. The more savage the punishment, the greater would be the gratification of a people conditioned to bloody and painful legal retribution. The annual carnival was about to commence, and the principal performers had arrived.

[1] Thomas Franklyn, of the Parish of St Margaret, King's Lynn, was charged with riotous assembly and assault, following a pitched battle in Thornham, on 31st December 1783, between a large gang of local smugglers and Excise Officers and Dragoons. A detailed account of the career of Franklyn is the subject of a later chapter.

THE THETFORD ASSIZES
Thursday 17th March to Tuesday 22nd March, 1785

The innkeepers, traders and shop-keepers of Thetford, for centuries past, had regarded the week of the Assizes as the most important annual event in the business calendar. There were nineteen inns within the town at this time, providing a total of two hundred and forty-three guest beds, according to a contemporary War Office national survey.[1] Most of the rooms and stables had been booked in advance, to accommodate the Circuit Judge and his entourage of clerks and recorders[2], together with twelve members of the Grand Jury, thirty-six Petty Jurors[3], various Prosecution and Defence attorneys and solicitors, and more than one hundred witnesses. On this occasion, there was also a large military presence, in view of the notoriety of two of the prisoners facing pro- secution. In addition, many Government officials representing the Treasury and the Boards of Customs and of Excise from London had gathered in the town to witness the crucial proceedings. The Bell was regarded as the town's superior inn, and accommodated the Judge, Mr. Justice Ashurst, and the Grand Jury; the other principal establishments were the George, the White Hart, the King's Head, the Fleece, the Red Lion and the King's Arms[4]. On the streets, market stalls, pedlars and entertainers appeared; visitors flocked to the town to enjoy the event and

---

[1] Military barracks were not a feature of eighteenth century England, and billeting of soldiers was imposed upon the owners of inns throughout the country. For this reason, the War Office regularly updated its lists of inns suitable for the accommodation of soldiers and especially horses.

[2] Every year, during March and April, the Circuit Judge and his entourage travelled to the Assizes in each of the counties of Bedfordshire, Buckinghamshire, Huntingdonshire, Cambridgeshire, Norfolk and Suffolk, on what was known as the 'Norfolk Circuit'.

[3] The Grand Jury consisted of twelve appointed men, chosen from the County's aristocracy and major landowners. The purpose of this Jury was to determine whether the evidence against those accused was sufficient to allow the matter to proceed to trial. The Petty Jury consisted of a panel of thirty-six men, chosen from the County's list of parliamentary voters; twelve of these men would hear the evidence for and against each of the accused, and pronounce a final verdict of either guilt or innocence.

[4] The other twelve inns providing accommodation and stabling were:- The Crown, The Admiral Keppel, the Green Dragon, the Black Horse, the Angel, the Black Boy, the White Horse, the Spread Eagle, the Dolphin, the Carpenters' Arms, the Star and the Anchor.

the carnival atmosphere. For the prisoners, locked deep inside a stinking hell-hole where conditions were primitive even by eighteenth-century standards, their continuing ordeals were set to enter another, and for some, a final phase.

Outside the town gaol, a large and boisterous crowd had gathered, to pay the gaoler for the privilege of gaining admission to the cold, damp and dark interior, for the purpose of witnessing the degradation of, in particular, the prisoners charged with the more violent and the most publicised crimes. Kemball and Gunton were popular exhibits, as was the highway murderer James Cliffen. Groups of spectators were admitted, at the cost of sixpence apiece, to the dungeon, where they were led down ten well-worn, irregular stone steps to a tiny unventilated cell in which all eighteen male prisoners were confined. In the women's dungeon, the insane antics of Elizabeth Forster, soon to face trial for alleged arson, provided further amusement for the ghoulish spectators. At the expiry of their allocated viewing time, they returned to the clear air at street level, fully satisfied with the costly entertainment provided by a profiteering gaoler and the unwilling prisoners in his custody.

At nine o'clock in the morning of Thursday 17th March, Mr Justice Ashurst[1] and his entourage assembled with great ceremony inside the Courtroom of the Guildhall[2]; members of the Grand and Petty Juries were duly sworn in, while the public area filled quickly to capacity. The Norfolk Lent Assizes for the year 1785 were about to commence. The first prisoner was called and Joseph Buttisant, a labourer from Felmingham, was brought from the town gaol dungeon[3] to stand trial. He was accused of stealing from Clement King, farmer, of North Walsham, one sheep, valued at twenty-five shillings. The Jury found him guilty and the Judge pronounced sentence; Buttisant was to be hanged by

[1] Sir William Henry Ashurst, 1725-1807, appointed Judge 1770, presided over Assizes on the Norfolk Circuit throughout the 1780s. A diehard reactionary, he left for execution more convicts at County Assizes than most of his contemporaries.
[2] The Guildhall and Courtroom in use in 1785 was the original medieval building of flint construction, which was demolished and replaced in 1799, and again in 1902, on the same site overlooking the Market Place. The statue of Justice which adorns the North gable of the present day building is the only remaining feature from the Guildhall of 1785, having been added to the original medieval structure in 1690.
[3] The town gaol was not part of the Guildhall, but was located in a separate building in Old Market Street.

the neck until dead. The bewildered young man was led away, to be replaced by the next prisoner, Robert Cademy of Tattersett. He was indicted with feloniously stealing twelve ewes, valued at four guineas, from John Hall, farmer, of the same village. Cademy also received the sentence of death from the Judge. The morning's business in Court was completed when Thomas Lond and John Booty, labourers from Kirby Cane, were both found guilty of stealing seven live hogs from Jeremiah Aldrich. The Judge sentenced both men to be transported[1] 'beyond the Seas for a term of seven years'.

In the afternoon session, John Clamp, a labourer from Stanhoe, was tried for stealing two sheep from William Meck, a farmer from the same village. Clamp was found guilty, and again the Circuit Judge produced his black cap to pronounce sentence of death. William Newland, for forgery, was similarly sentenced; Mary Barker, for theft and burglary at a house in Earsham, was fined and committed to six months' hard labour in the County Gaol at Norwich Castle. By the end of the first day at the Assizes, seven prisoners had been tried for various crimes. All seven had been found guilty and of these, four had been sentenced to hang. They were all returned, for the duration of the Assizes, to the town prison, where the Gaoler was able to offer the added attraction of exhibiting to public gaze and curiosity a quartet of capitally convicted criminals. During the next two days' proceedings, a further eleven prisoners were tried. Of these, Robert Randall, for 'robbing and firing a pistol at Robert Haman of Easton and Heber Watts of Matishall on the King's highway in the parish of Costessy', John Flint for stealing a mare at Emneth, and John Ferrett for burglary at a house in Yarmouth, were all sentenced to be hanged. Thomas Sparshall of Beetley, for stealing an ass, was to be

---

[1] In the early years of transportation, from the beginning of the 17th century up to the 1770s, convicts were usually sent to the plantations in the American colonies of Virginia and Massachusetts. At the outbreak of the American War of Independence in 1777, the Government was forced to look elsewhere for a suitable outlet for its unwanted criminals. Throughout the 1780s, English prisons and the floating hulks overflowed with convicts awaiting transportation, as the backlog grew at an alarming rate. It was not until the end of the decade that a new colonial acquisition, on the very edge of the world, was chosen as the dumping ground. In 1787, the first fleet left for Botany Bay, laden with the first of an estimated total of 160,000 convicts who would eventually be despatched to the Australian continent.

transported for life, and John Garner of East Dereham, for stealing five pigs, and subsequently selling them at the Dereham live-stock market, was sentenced to seven years' transportation.

The fourth day of business at the Assizes began on Monday 21st March. The townspeople of Thetford were in a rare state of excitement and anticipation at the approach of the trials of the infamous smugglers. Already, seven men had been sentenced to hang and four others faced an uncertain future in a brutal penal colony abroad. There was every reason to expect that the savage sentencing would continue at the hands of the repressive Circuit Judge.

By early morning, the streets of Thetford were crowded with visitors and spectators, many of whom had a direct interest in the outcome of the trials. From London and King's Lynn came officials representing the Board of Customs; from various parts of the County of Norfolk came twenty-three prosecution witnesses, who had been involved in one way or another with the events in Old Hunstanton village the previous September; from Snettisham came the distraught figure of Phoebe Green, widow of the murdered Customs Officer. Most importantly, from all parts of Norfolk came the smuggling fraternity, in great numbers, with the sole intention of intimidating the panel of Jurors who would deliver the vital verdicts. Their collective presence could not have failed to cause the jurors many moments of inward reflection, and a permanent state of outright fear. The probability of violent acts of revenge by aggrieved smugglers and their sympathisers was a prospect too terrifying to contemplate; only a brave or foolish man would seriously consider casting a vote in favour of sending high-ranking smugglers to their deaths.

The prosecution, as we have seen, was apprehensive about the composition of the jury and had investigated thoroughly the background of each individual member of the panel. After challenging the presence of four jurors suspected of being involved with, or sympathetic to, the smuggling trade, Mr Murphy, the Prosecution Counsel, settled for the following twelve Norfolk men:-

Joseph Cole, Upwell	John Turner, Gt Ellingham
Benjamin Frost, Shouldham	Thomas Steward, Gt Ellingham
George Leech, Foulden	Robert Payne, Attleborough
Thomas Stocking, Hilborough	William Chapman, Attleborough

Francis Barsham, Wimbotsham   Ezekiel Read, Bridgham

Robert Brooke, Carbrooke   James Nurse, Gt Hockham

Significantly, none of the selected jurors resided in a coastal region of the county and none came from the immediate area of Old Hunstanton.

The selected jury's first task of the day was to listen to evidence against another alleged murderer, James Cliffen. Despite being manacled with wrist and leg irons, Cliffen had to be restrained by two gaolers throughout his appearance in court. He shouted abuse at the witnesses, the judge and the jury. He protested vehemently his innocence of the charges levelled against him that, on the King's Highway at Yaxham, he had robbed an old man named Peter Seaman of a purse containing two gold guineas and one half-crown, and that in the course of the robbery, he had beaten his victim with a heavy club, giving him a mortal fracture on the left side of the skull. Peter Seaman died from the inflicted wounds eleven days later.[1] The jury listened to the evidence of several witnesses and returned a verdict of guilty on both counts; Cliffen was sentenced to be hanged by the neck until dead on Thursday 24th March at the Castle ditches in Norwich. Thereafter, his body would be taken to Badley Moor near Yaxham, where it would hang in an iron cage from the arm of a gibbet, in a prominent position close to the public highway.

The members of the jury had accepted the evidence against James Cliffen and had unanimously pronounced him guilty; the same men would next concentrate their minds upon the trials of the smugglers.

THE TRIAL OF KEMBALL AND GUNTON
Thetford, Monday 21st March 1785

Kemball and Gunton were brought from the gaol house to stand trial firstly for their part in the murder of William Green the Customs Officer.

---

[1] The incident occurred on the night of 11th February 1785 in a lane close to Yaxham parish church. After the alleged assault and robbery, Cliffen was pursued by a 'hue and cry'; he reached Dereham and sought refuge in the Green Man public house, where his suspicious manner and his blood-stained frock-coat attracted the attention of the landlord, Mr Goddard Wigg. Cliffen, who previously had served a term of hard labour on the prison hulks in the Thames Estuary, was taken from the Green Man to a local Justice of the Peace, who in turn committed him to Norwich Castle Gaol to await trial at the Thetford Assizes.

The court room, which had been busily occupied throughout the Assizes, was now full to capacity. Kemball was indicted with having 'on the 26th September last, at Old Hunstanton, wilfully murdered William Green by discharging a gun loaded with gun-powder and one leaden bullet[1], to, at and upon the said William Green, wounding him mortally in the left side of the belly, to a length of twelve inches and a breadth of half an inch, of which wound he languished to the next day and died'. Gunton was indicted for his part in the same murder, 'by being present, and by aiding and assisting in the same murder'.

Mr Murphy, for the prosecution, opened the case and Thomas Mitchell, the Customs Officer from Wells, was the first witness to be called upon to give evidence. He gave a detailed account of his part of the proceedings, from the moment he first received information at the Wells Customs House about the intention to land smuggled goods at Hunstanton, to the time of the arrests of Kemball and Gunton some ten hours later. Particularly detailed was his account of the shootings in the lane leading to Old Hunstanton beach; he was positive that he had seen and identified Kemball, by the flashes of light cast by gunfire, during the first volley which had killed the Dragoon and had mortally wounded the Customs Officer. Mitchell also confirmed that, when Kemball was arrested, he was in possession of two recently discharged carbines and seven lead musket balls, all of which material evidence was produced in court. Christopher Stangroom, the Excise Officer, was the next witness to give testimony; he too stated that he had seen Kemball, and Gunton also, behind the lane's hedgerow in the act of firing. The defence counsel challenged Stangroom's ability to identify positively the accused men, in view of the fact that the shootings took place at night. Stangroom countered that the visibility that night was such that he could see clearly for a distance of thirty of forty yards, and that he was only fifteen yards distant from Kemball and Gunton when they opened fire. Stangroom

---

[1] In the 18th century, all fire-arms, whether pistols, muskets or carbines, were muzzle-loading, single shot weapons which necessitated a time-consuming re-loading process after every firing, involving priming the firing pan and the barrel with gunpowder and a single lead ball, with the help of a ram rod. Infantry in the British Regiments of Foot were trained and drilled to such a high standard of expertise with the musket that a firing rate of three, and even four, rounds per minute was achieved. Sea-faring smugglers and pirates preferred the luxury, which they could well afford, of multiple weaponry, slung from leather body straps, which could contain as many as a dozen primed and loaded single-shot pistols.

then recalled his conversation with William Green in Clare's farm-house, whilst the Customs Officer lay on his death-bed. Stangroom claimed that Green had said, 'My business is done; I shall not recover'. 'We have taken William Kemball and two of his men', replied Stangroom, to which Willam Green responded, 'William Kemball was the man that shot me, I am sure of it'.

Further witnesses were called. Lieutenant Wheelock testified that when Kemball was arrested in the yard of the Cutter alehouse, he was in possession of two recently discharged carbines and seven lead musket balls. Private Matthews and Thomas Jarvis of the Excise confirmed this account, while Sergeant Major Leishman described the arrest of Gunton, who similarly was found in possession of incriminating weaponry.

Thomas Williams was next to take his stand in the witness box. He recounted in full the events from the time the *Lively* sailed out of Dunkirk with its contraband cargo, to the time he was arrested in Hunstanton shortly after the shootings in the lane. The Prosecution Counsel, Mr Murphy, ensured that his key witness, having turned King's evidence, should give as detailed and incriminating an account as possible to establish Kemball's guilt. Williams made frequent reference to Kemball's reckless, irrational and violent mood following the seizure of his smuggled goods on the beach by the Excise party. Kemball had personally issued eight of his crew-members with loaded fire-arms, together with instructions to use them. He had threatened to kill anyone who disobeyed his orders, which were to rescue the seized goods at whatever cost. It was Kemball, insisted Williams, who had given the order to fire on the soldiers and preventive men in the lane, and it was Kemball who had fired the first shot.

The Defence Counsel, before calling his own witnesses, attempted to discredit Williams' evidence by drawing attention to his alleged dubious status. 'Were you not taken before a Magistrate, accused of murder and committed for trial, following the shootings in the lane in Old Hunstanton on the night of 25th/26th September 1784'? 'Yes', replied Williams. 'Is it not a fact', continued the Defence, 'that you spare your own life by giving evidence against your two colleagues who now stand trial?' 'Yes', replied Williams once again. It was standard practice for the defence to cast doubt upon the reliability of a witness who had turned against his own colleagues and was prepared to assist in their prosecution, in the cause of self preservation. Defence Counsel then called the first of its own witnesses. John Smyth, an agricultural labourer from Old Hunstanton, gave his own version of events. On the night in question, he had been working late, it being harvest-time, storing grain in the barns at Ringstead Yards Farm for his employer, Daniel Frostwick.[1] Smyth alleged that he left the farm at about one o'clock in the morning, had walked to Hunstanton and arrived at the Cutter alehouse at about a quarter to two. He had heard no shootings in the village up to this time. On entering the Cutter, he had ordered a glass of gin and had spoken to William Kemball, who was sitting in a chair drinking beer. At about 2 o'clock, Smyth alleged, he had left the Cutter, where Kemball was still drinking, to return to his lodgings nearby, when almost immediately he had heard the sound of a volley of eight or ten muskets being fired in the vicinity of the beach lane. It was therefore impossible, Smyth emphasised, that Kemball had any part whatsoever in the shootings and subsequent murders.

It is almost certain that John Smyth had been either handsomely bribed or seriously intimidated into giving Kemball a strong alibi. Thomas Cooper, landlord of the Cutter, confirmed Smyth's account; he too stated, in evidence, that the unarmed Kemball had been drinking in the alehouse at the time of the shootings. A third defence witness was called in the person of Thomas Cutting, head turnkey at Norwich Castle prison. Cutting, as we have seen, had profited financially by providing Kemball and Gunton with superior accommodation and privileges during their confinement at the Castle prison. No doubt the gaoler would receive further reward for his supportive evidence in favour of the two smugglers, by stating that the prosecution's main witness, Thomas Williams, had confided that his captain, William Kemball, 'knew nothing about the alleged murders and was not in the lane at the time of the shootings'. Yet another witness, Peter Jacques Renuck, a native of Dunkirk, was produced by the Defence to cast serious doubts about both the character and reliability of Thomas Williams. Renuck claimed that Williams was a 'common murderer' who had sailed on board the pirate ship *Fearnought* under the command of the notorious North Sea pirate

---

[1] This is the same Daniel Frostwick who was the father of Phoebe Green and father-in-law to the murdered Customs Officer.

Captain Daniel Fall[1], whose raids had in recent years brought terror and suffering to the inhabitants of coastal villages in the Cromer neighbourhood. Although Williams fiercely denied having had any association with the pirate, it remained to be seen whether the jury would be influenced by the serious allegation.

Judge Ashurst then summed up the evidence on both sides. As a general rule, he stated, evidence given by accomplices who turn King's evidence, should be treated with caution. However, in this particular case, Williams' evidence had been confirmed by Stangroom and a number of Dragoon officers and men; in addition, the evidence produced by the prosecution amounted to 'a good body of evidence'. On the other hand, the evidence for the defence delivered in particular by Thomas Cooper of the alehouse and John Smyth the farm worker was inconsistent with that of the Dragoons. The Judge, nevertheless, left the Jurors in no doubt that he expected a guilty verdict.

The twelve members of the Jury retired to a private room to consider the evidence they had heard and to reach a unanimous verdict. Three hours elapsed before they re-appeared to announce their astonishing decision; both Kemball and Gunton were pronounced 'not guilty'. It is, of course, impossible to describe with certainty the deliberations which had taken place behind the closed doors of the jury's chamber. The fact that the twelve men took such a long time to deliver their verdicts suggests disagreement within their ranks; some jurors may have supported, initially at least, a verdict of guilty. Alternatively, there may have been unanimous support for an acquittal from the beginning; the three hour 'debate' may have been a smokescreen, to give the impression to the world outside that serious consideration was being given to all the points raised by the prosecution and defence. However, one certainty remains; some, if not all, of the jurors had been intimidated, directly or indirectly, by the smuggling fraternity and the community generally into returning a 'not guilty' verdict. The prosecution was outraged by the

---

[1] Daniel Fall inflicted a reign of terror upon numerous isolated village communities on the coasts of Yorkshire, Lincolnshire and Norfolk during the 1770s and 1780s. His crewmen specialised in violent armed robbery, house-breaking, burning, looting, rape and murder. The Pirate Captain was never brought to justice, although eleven of his crew were less fortunate. In March 1781, whilst plundering houses in the Norfolk coastal village of West Runton, they were apprehended by the Press Gang and impressed into the service of the Royal Navy.

jurors' decision and Mr Murphy, the Prosecution Counsel, announced that 'if a Norfolk Jury was determined not to convict smugglers guilty of the most atrocious crimes, there was an end of all justice'.

For the second trial, due to commence on the morning of the following day, for the murder of Private William Webb, the present Jury would be dismissed and twelve new members empanelled.

THE TRIAL OF GUNTON AND KEMBALL
Tuesday, 22nd March, 1785, Thetford

Immediately after the verdict was announced, a meeting was convened hastily at the Bell Inn. The London-based prosecution and its advisors were called together by George Litchfield, chief solicitor to the Customs Board, to discuss and decide upon their next move. In reality, the Londoners were out of their depth in rural Norfolk, a peripheral county where the King's laws were open to local interpretation. It was a county where even the clergy refused to speak or preach against the activities and even the atrocities committed by smugglers. Parson Woodforde, rector of the parish of Weston Longville in the heart of the county, was regularly in receipt of tubs of brandy and bags of tea, delivered to the parsonage back door in the dead of night. His conscience was clear and untroubled by such illicit transactions. On the contrary, his Diaries[1] contain many references to his part in the illegal trafficking, and more particularly, his receiving smuggled goods, without a hint of secular or religious guilt. 'Andrews the Smuggler brought me this night, at about eleven o'clock', wrote the Parson on 29 March 1777, 'a bagg of Hyson Tea, six pounds weight. He frightened us a little by whistling under the Parlour Window just as we were going to bed. I gave him some Geneva and paid him for the tea at 10/6d per pound.....£3.3.0.'

In the earlier years of the century, a more prominent Norfolk man, Sir Robert Walpole, who was for twenty years Prime Minister in all but name, was a regular receiver of smuggled goods. His Norfolk residence, Houghton Hall, was visited frequently by James Swanton, a smuggler from Wells, who provided fine imported linen and wines free from

---

[1] Parson James Woodforde, 1740-1803, Rector of Weston Longville from 1774 until his death. The larger part of his Diaries describes his daily life in Norfolk from 1776 onwards.

customs duties. Elsewhere, on one remarkable occasion, Walpole commissioned the assistance of an Admiralty launch to rescue a large quantity of smuggled claret, burgundy and champagne from the busy hands of Customs Officers at the pool of London, close by Customs headquarters. The illicit cargo was safely conveyed up river to Walpole's grateful possession at Westminster.

Against this background, the prosecution must have felt isolated and powerless. If the parochial Norfolk mentality was in itself a difficult obstacle to overcome, then even more difficult was the county's obsessive hatred of Customs and Excise officials, who were viewed as tyrannical agents of central government, armed with unlimited powers of search and entry into private property. These powers were frequently abused by over-zealous revenue officers, and accusations of violence, theft and extortion were routinely levelled against them. The popularly held belief that officers of Customs and Excise were beyond redemption, beneath contempt and consequently unworthy of protection by the law, may well have been prejudicial to the prosecution's case during the first trial, and the omens were not favourable for its chances of successful convictions at the second trial.

At the Bell Inn, the prosecution debated the composition of the jury who would sit in judgement at the next day's trial; indeed, it was the only topic on the agenda. All agreed that the presentation of evidence at the first trial could not have been bettered and that the defence witnesses were perjurers. In fact, the only ingredient absent from the first trial was a jury of twelve honest and fearless men who could be relied upon to deliver a just and proper verdict. Could such a body of men be found in this lawless county? It seemed unlikely; nevertheless, the names of four local men from the town of Thetford were added to the original panel of thirty-six jurors. Messengers were despatched to their places of abode, commanding each of them to attend the Assize Court the following morning. The newly empanelled men were intended to form a nucleus within the ranks of the jury, in order to encourage their fellow jurors to reach an honest and appropriate decision, without prejudice against authority and without bias toward the smuggling brotherhood. In the event, it proved to be a last desperate gamble which was easily countered by the defence, because the final panel of twelve men contained the names of John Gooch and Thomas Syder, both of whom had been

A detail from the original document listing the 36 jurors empanelled to serve at the Thetford Assizes in March 1785, compiled by Robert Whincop.

The names of three jurors, William Hardy, John Gooch and Thomas Syder, have been underlined and the capital letter C for 'Challenge' added to each name.

challenged and excluded from participating in the first jury on account of their alleged and suspected direct connection with the smuggling trade.

To the Assize court house on the morning of Tuesday, 22nd March, Kemball and Gunton were once again delivered from the town gaol, in order to stand trial for their part in the murder of Private William Webb of the 15th Regiment of Light Dragoons. Andrew Gunton was indicted with having 'on 26th September last, wilfully murdered William Webb by discharging a gun loaded with gunpowder and two leaden bullets to, at and upon the said William Webb, giving him one mortal wound four inches in length and half an inch in breadth upon the belly, of which mortal wound he instantly died'. William Kemball was indicted for his part in the same murder, 'by being present, aiding and assisting'.

As on the previous day, the Court room was crowded with officials, jurors, witnesses and spectators. At centre stage were the twelve new Jurors[1] who would decide the outcome of a murder trial of vital importance. The evidence presented by both prosecution and defence was almost identical to that of the previous day's trial, and an air of inevitability was apparent, despite the changes in jury personnel. As before, Judge Ashurst, summing up, emphasised the credibility of the prosecution's strong circumstantial evidence, and expressed clearly his expectation of a just and proper verdict from the jury.

For Kemball and Gunton, waiting apprehensively in a Court house ante room for the second time in successive days while the jury discussed the evidence, and ultimately their fates, the minutes passed agonisingly slowly. The longer the deliberations lasted, the more their confidence, hope and expectations grew. Who can say with any certainty what course was taken in the argument for and against the defendants? As the minutes turned to hours, emotions within the Court room displayed the extremes of anxiety and optimism, fear and hope. After three hours, the jury indicated that a unanimous verdict had been reached. Court officials re-assembled, two visibly trembling smugglers were brought back to the

---

[1] The Prosecution's newly empanelled Jurors, all from Thetford, were Henry Roberts, William Roberts, John Ellis and John Sheering. The other eight, from various parts of the County, were:-

Thomas Syder, from Banham	James Gooch, from North Lopham
Thomas Collison, from Beechamwell	John Foulsham, from Attleborough
Francis King, from Northwold	John Jolly, from Banham
John Palmer, from Rushford	James Murton, from Blo Norton

dock and the jury foreman was asked, firstly, whether the defendant Andrew Gunton was found 'guilty' or 'not guilty'. Total silence in the room was broken by the foreman's pronouncement: 'Not guilty'. Reaction from the public gallery was both noisy and mixed; in a voice barely audible above the general cacophony, the Judge asked for the verdict on William Kemball. Again came the reply: 'Not guilty', prompting an outburst of uncontrolled excitement. The verdicts were relayed to the mob waiting in the market square outside the Court house, where impatience gave way immediately to vociferous approval.

Inside the Court house, there was obvious relief on the faces of the two defendants, their witnesses and supporters. Other emotions were in evidence; Phoebe Green, the murdered Customs Officer's widow, was utterly distraught. She would return to her home in Snettisham to continue the fight for justice. Christopher Stangroom, who was instrumental in capturing the acquitted smugglers in Old Hunstanton village, was incensed by the verdicts; he too would return to Snettisham to campaign for a satisfactory conclusion. Customs Officers, Excise Officers and Army personnel stared with a combination of contempt and disbelief in the direction of the jurors responsible for such an appalling miscarriage of justice[1]. Meanwhile, the proceedings at the Lent Assizes for the County of Norfolk for the year 1785 were formally terminated by the Judge's traditional show of leniency towards some of the convicts condemned to die. Before he left town to travel to the next Assizes on the circuit at Bury St Edmunds in the neighbouring county of Suffolk, Judge Ashurst reprieved three of the eight capitally convicted felons from the death sentence. Instead, John Clamp, Joseph Buttisant and John Flint would be transported for life to the African continent. It was, nevertheless, merely a mock display of clemency: having been spared from death at the end of a rope, they would be shipped to an island in the River Gambia where they would experience a living death in the form of a hostile climate and rampant pestilence. They would almost certainly die sooner rather than later from malnutrition, or malignant fever, or at the hands of hostile natives.

The remaining five condemned convicts were left for execution.

---

[1] According to a report in the *Norfolk Chronicle*, four of the jurors were in favour of convicting the smugglers, while eight favoured an acquittal. It must be assumed that the four Thetford jurors, empanelled at the eleventh hour, argued unsuccessfully for a conviction, but resigned themselves eventually to the majority view.

DISPOSAL OF THE PRISONERS
Wednesday, 23 March 1785

On the morning of 23rd March 1785, all the prisoners convicted at the Assizes were collected from the Gaol house at Thetford and returned on prison carts to the County Gaol at Norwich Castle, to await execution or transportation, or to serve gaol sentences. In addition, Kemball and Gunton were also returned to the Castle, following their re-arrest by one of the Sheriff of Norfolk's officers immediately after their acquittal. Both men were detained under Writs of Capias prepared by the Customs' solicitor in case of their acquittal, on smuggling as opposed to murder charges. They had escaped the hangman's noose, but they were not yet free men.

James Cliffen, the Yaxham highway murderer, was the first prisoner to be disposed of according to law. After just one night in a cell at Norwich Castle, he was carried on a black-draped, horse-drawn cart to the gallows on Castle Hill, accompanied by gaolers, the hangman and a priest. A death bell tolled mournfully as he was conveyed the short distance to his place of execution. With considerable defiance, Cliffen made good use of the traditional opportunity to address the enormous crowd of spectators which always assembled at the Castle ditches to witness executions.[1] He protested his innocence of the crime for which he was about to die and reminded the blood-thirsty hordes assembled before him that there were two prisoners currently lodged in the Castle prison who should take his place at the gallows. This was a clear reference to Kemball and Gunton. Even if Cliffen were guilty, and the overwhelming evidence given at his trial suggests that the verdict was correct, it was outrageous that he should have been capitally convicted by

---

[1] Executions were always carried out in public at this time, and were a popular form of mass entertainment, attracting spectators from all parts of the County, from all classes of society. They attracted also large numbers of legitimate traders and peddlers, who cashed in on the opportunity to sell their wares in the crowded city streets, and inevitably hordes of less legitimate opportunists in the form of pickpockets, fraudsters and prostitutes. Worthy emotions such as public revulsion or sympathy were not in evidence; indeed, moments before the fatal drop, the popular cry of 'Hats off' was traditionally chanted, not as a mark of respect to the victim, but to afford those spectators at the back of the crowd a better, unimpeded view. It was not until 1869 that executions were removed from public view and conducted behind closed doors in prison yards.

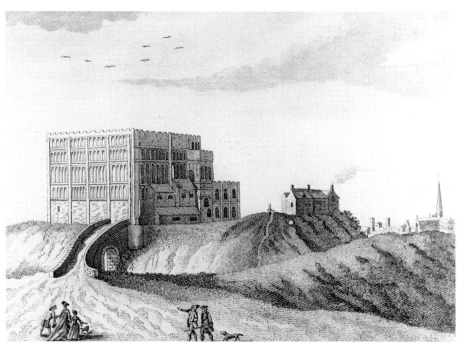

Norwich Castle Prison, 1785.
Public executions were carried out at the foot of the stone bridge, in the presence of large numbers of spectators who travelled great distances to witness the entertainment.

An 18th century public execution from a Thomas Bewick woodcut.

the twelve Jurors who, on the same day, acquitted Kemball and Gunton despite the compelling evidence given against the two smugglers. The Editor of the *Norfolk Chronicle* criticised in strong terms both juries for failing to convict Kemball and Gunton; he even published the names of the individual jurors concerned, in an attempt to embarrass them publicly.

The gesture was clearly of no consequence to James Cliffen. After he had uttered his last words of defiance to the impatient mob, a noose, which was suspended by a length of rope from a horizontal cross-beam, was placed around his neck by the hangman. A black hood was pulled down over his face, the horses attached to the cart on which he stood were sharply prodded, and Cliffen was left swinging from side to side at the rope's end. Death was not instantaneous; it took a full fifteen minutes of slow strangulation before Cliffen finally expired. In some cases at the gallows, friends or family were permitted to tug at the waist and legs of the suspended victim, in order to precipitate death and thereby reduce prolonged suffering. Cliffen was allowed no such dubious privilege.

After an hour, when the enormous crowd of satisfied spectators had begun to disperse into the city's streets to sample alternative entertainment and gratification, the corpse of James Cliffen was lowered from the gallows and returned to the Castle on the horse-drawn cart. Two days later, on Easter Saturday, it was conveyed to a site on the edge of Badley Moor, about one and a half miles to the east of Yaxham village, where the murder was committed. A gibbet, consisting of a sturdy upright post and cross-beam, was erected in a prominent position visible from the public highway and Cliffen's body, which had been liberally daubed with tar as a preservative, was placed within a body-shaped iron cage and suspended from the gibbet's arm. The revolting spectacle of a slowly rotting corpse was created deliberately to deter others from criminal pursuit[1]. In practice, the Badley Moor gibbet became a prominent Norfolk landmark, attracting voyeuristic visitors from far and near. Parson James Woodforde of Weston Longville was amongst the first of the ghoulish voyeurs to travel to the Moor. Carrion crows, rooks and magpies had already begun to disfigure and feed off the corpse by

---

[1] Gibbeting was a fairly common practice in England at this time, as it had been since the early medieval period, especially for convicted highway murderers. It was finally abolished by Act of Parliament in 1834.

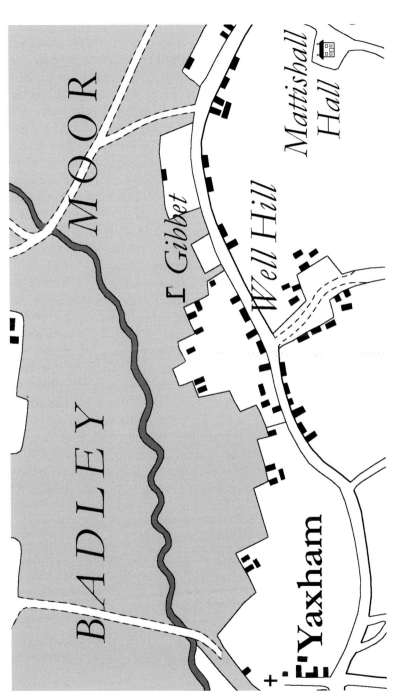

Detail from Faden's map of Norfolk, 1797, showing Cliffen's gibbet on the edge of Badley Moor. Faden recorded a total of nine gibbets on his Norfolk map.

the time the Parson decided upon a leisurely journey. 'On April 4th, after breakfast', he wrote in his Diary, 'being fine weather, I took a ride (and Will, my servant, with me) through Hockering and North Tuddenham to Badley Moor where Cliffen hangs in chains'. Shockingly, given his status as a man of the cloth, he complained not about the barbaric spectacle of which he was a willing viewer, but of the poor state of the roads in the vicinity. 'Most shocking road all around where Cliffen stands', he wrote; 'for some way, I thought we should have been mired'.

The execution of Cliffen was followed nine days later by the disposal of the four remaining capitally convicted prisoners. On Saturday 2nd April, 1785, the citizens of Norwich assembled once again in great numbers to witness the mass execution of William Newland for forgery, Robert Cademy for sheep stealing, Robert Randall for highway robbery and John Ferrett for burglary. William Newland almost succeeded in escaping the noose; a few days before his execution, having broken free from both leg irons and prison cell, he reached the top of the Castle walls before a fellow prisoner raised the alarm. A further seven convicts remained in the Castle, awaiting transportation. Of these, John Garner of East Dereham was granted a free pardon as a result of a successful petition to the King made by the principal inhabitants of his home town.[1] The other six lingered on in the Castle because of difficulties faced by the authorities in effecting the punishment of transportation. North America had recently gained its independence, the Australian continent was not yet a convict-dumping colony, and parliamentary opposition to sending further convicts to the fever-ridden swamps of the river Gambia caused a temporary cessation to the policy of punitive expatriation. With the exception of John Clamp of Stanhoe, who like

---

[1] The petition relied heavily upon the certain distress and destitution which would have befallen Garner's wife and six young children in the event of the bread-winner's transportation. The Home Office was regularly in receipt of such petitions which, despite their emotive content and appeals for mercy on compassionate grounds, were almost always rejected. Garner's petition had the considerable advantage of being signed by a number of prominent, wealthy and influential members of society, particularly local gentry and clergy, and this endorsement proved to be decisive. Also helpful to Garner's cause was his co-operation in raising the alarm to foil William Newland's attempted escape from the Castle. Within a few months of his reprieve, Garner was again committed to the Castle, charged with stealing a bay mare. After six months in prison awaiting trial, he was blessed once more with good fortune by being acquitted at the Thetford Assizes in March 1786.

The Badley Moor Gibbet

William Faden's late 18th century map of Norfolk clearly marks the site of the Gibbet on Badley Moor with a simplified symbol depicting an upright post, crossbeam and hanging corpse. The survey for the Map was carried out in 1792, seven years after the body was first taken to the Moor, and clearly the grim spectacle had lost none of its visual impact. All remains of the Gibbet have now vanished, yet, curiously, a Georgian farmhouse, which stands some 200 yards west of the site, bears to this day the name Clifton Villa.

Over 100 years later, in September 1898, letters of curious content were published in two Norwich newspapers. The letters contained the bizarre story of the discovery of a human skull believed to be that of James Cliffen. Mr Henry Mallet wrote that, as a boy, he remembered seeing the ghastly remains of Cliffen's skeleton hanging from the gibbet on Badley Moor in the 1830s. He further remembered his mother recounting how, in the 1790s, parish boys would throw stones at the corpse until the putrid flesh was literally cut or knocked away. Henry Mallet claimed that his cousin cut down the skeleton from the gibbet, as late as the 1850s, and buried the remains in a field nearby. A few years later, the bones and skull were ploughed up by an agricultural labourer, and the skull eventually came into the possession of a Mr Chaplin, who informed the newspapers of his acquisition.

The same newspapers claimed that the remains of Cliffen's iron gibbet were to be seen in Norwich Castle Museum. The remains are still held there, although not on public display.

Garner received a free pardon, the remaining convicted prisoners remained in the Castle until July 1785; thereafter, their names disappear from records and it is likely that they were forced to enlist in the Army as an alternative to transportation, although their ultimate fates remain uncertain.

Equally uncertain were the fates of Kemball and Gunton, although initially fortune continued to favour their careers. A combination of administrative bungling and legal indecision, over an eighteen-month period, allowed them to adopt a cavalier and derisive attitude to the Law, its institutions and its courts, with the abandon of men who had cheated the hangman and who believed that they were at liberty to act as they pleased. At first, however, determined efforts were made, especially by the murdered Customs Officer's widow Phoebe Green, to continue the fight for justice. Within a few days of returning home to Snettisham from the Assizes at Thetford, the determined widow travelled to the Customs House at King's Lynn. There she persuaded the Customs Collector to attempt to commence further proceedings against Kemball and Gunton. The following week, the *Norfolk Chronicle* newspaper printed a story claiming that the two smugglers would be brought to trial again and would appear before a special jury at the Summer Assizes in Norwich later in the year. However, there was no legal precedent for a retrial, for the same offence, of persons previously found 'not guilty', and all hopes of bringing the smugglers before another jury on murder charges were quickly dashed. Phoebe Green's only consolation was the unusually generous pension granted to her for life by the traditionally parsimonious Board of Customs. In recognition of the fact that 'her late husband had lost his life in the actual execution of his duty, was a good and active officer, and that his wife and children were left entirely destitute', Phoebe Green was awarded the sum of £15 per annum, together with an annual sum of £2-10-0 for each of her five children until they attained the age of fifteen years.

Kemball and Gunton remained in Norwich Castle until the morning of 12 April 1785, when they were taken by post-chaise to London to face charges of smuggling at the Court of Exchequer at Westminster. Exchequer trials were not concerned with murder or assault of revenue officials, but with alleged attempts to defraud either the Customs or the Excise. Kemball and Gunton had directed the landings of subsequently seized contraband goods on Old Hunstanton beach on the night of the murders, and the landings of these goods formed the basis of the prosecution they now faced.

Both smugglers appeared before the Barons of the Exchequer on 13 April 1785 on charges of bringing ashore goods and failing to pay the required import duty, calculated at the sum of £351. The prosecution demanded the statutory forfeit of three times that amount, arriving at a proposed fine of £1053[1]. In the absence of vital witnesses who failed to appear, possibly by chance but probably owing to intimidation, the prosecution was unable to prove its case in its entirety. Nevertheless, the Court was able to judge in favour of the prosecution for part of the contraband landed on Old Hunstanton beach and both smugglers were fined a reduced, although still substantial, sum of £303. The proceedings were not terminated, but adjourned to a later date in order to allow the prosecution to organise its witnesses. Kemball and Gunton's counsel applied for bail on behalf of his clients, which was granted; it was the last occasion that either man would be seen in an Exchequer Court, or any other English court of law. Furthermore, the two smugglers took their leave without even paying their respective fines, although immediate payment of bail set at £299 per man was levied as a condition of their release.[2]

The two smugglers walked out of the court room into the springtime sunshine of the streets of Westminster, free at last after seven months of uncertainty, incarceration and fear. The rigours of foetid prison cells in Norwich castle and Thetford gaol, the constant threat of the hangman's noose, and their battles for survival in the Assize and Exchequer courtrooms had all been negotiated successfully. Their considerable financial resources had enabled them to clear the final obstacle in their path to freedom, and the payment of bail was a small price to pay; neither man had any intention of honouring their commitment to return to face further justice. It is easy to imagine that their good luck was celebrated at great length and in some style in the taverns of Whitehall and the Strand. Nevertheless, their massive expenditure, on lawyers' fees,

---

[1] Such a fine would be the equivalent of well in excess of £100,000 in today's monetary terms.

[2] An indication of the wealth accumulated over the years by the two smugglers can be deduced from the fact that their lawyer paid instantly the huge sum of money to secure the release of his clients.

bribes for witnesses, gaolers' fees and bail, necessitated an early return to the business of smuggling. Within a few days of their release, they took a coach to Deal in Kent and set sail on a smuggling lugger, arriving in Calais towards the end of April 1785 to resume their lucrative lifestyle.

BACK IN BUSINESS
May 1785 to March 1786

By the end of May 1785, Kemball had returned to the business he knew best. Equipped with a new lugger named the *Rodney*, built to the same exacting specifications as his previous smuggling vessel, he resumed the illegal running of contraband to the coast of Norfolk, and possibly new target areas elsewhere on England's coasts. Documentary evidence in the form of recorded sightings by captains of Royal Navy and Customs cutters suggests that Kemball's renewed operations afloat were confined mainly to the coastline between Cromer and Yarmouth. Only once during the remaining months of 1785 did Kemball clash with the preventive authorities; in August, whilst attempting to land a cargo of brandy on Bacton beach, his long boat was captured and seized by the crew of the *Hunter* customs cutter. Kemball's response to this indignity was measured and tactful; instead of engaging in another bloody affray, he offered the second mate of the *Hunter*, Jacob Brazell, the handsome bribe of 30 tubs of cognac in return for the longboat. The deal was struck, to the satisfaction of smugglers and Customs men alike.[1]

By the end of the year, Kemball had returned to his old coastal haunts, and was again landing contraband on the beaches of Thornham, Holme and Old Hunstanton. At the same time, the Admiralty, free for once from the burden of overseas commitment and conflict, felt that it had sufficient vessels afloat to give greater assistance to the Revenue Service in the domestic war against smuggling at sea. Consequently, the Captains of four sloops and cruisers were ordered to patrol the North Sea coastline between Hollesley Bay and St Abbs Head. Of these vessels,

---

[1] Jacob Brazell and his captain Timothy Steward were dismissed from the Revenue service in December 1787 on the grounds of numerous alleged irregularities involving the acceptance of bribes from smugglers. Soon after his dismissal, Brazell purchased a public house in Great Yarmouth with the proceeds of his ill-gotten gains.

the Admiralty brig sloop the *Speedy*, which had been stationed at Great Yarmouth for much of 1784 and the early part of 1785 on smuggling patrol, now began to concentrate its efforts on the Old Hunstanton area. The *Speedy*, a 14-gun warship under the command of an energetic and ambitious Captain by the name of Josias Rogers[1], spent much of the latter half of 1785 at anchor in the Lynn Roads in The Wash, and patrolling off Hunstanton, Thornham and Brancaster, in the hope of apprehending Kemball. Captain Rogers' log book contains numerous references to possible and actual sightings of the smuggler whose capture had seemingly become an obsession. On 23 September 1785, Rogers recorded that 'whilst cruising 4 miles NNE of Hunstanton Light(house), and ¼ mile NNW of Farrier Beacon, I saw a large lugger under the high land of Hunstanton (i.e. the cliffs). At dusk, I put 10 men and 2 officers on board the tender *Lady Hammond*[2] and sent her in quest of the lugger. At 8 p.m. the tender found the lugger riding off Thornham Creek and sailed up alongside and boarded her. The lugger proved to be the *Revenge* from Dunkirk, owned by Robert Forshaw,[3] with 76 tubs of spirits on board, having landed most of her cargo two nights previously. My crew got the cargo and 13 smugglers on board the *Lady Hammond* and brought her to anchor alongside the *Speedy*'. Captain Rogers' log for the subsequent two days describes how he took great care to ensure that the seized tubs of alcohol were securely secreted behind lock and key on board the *Lady Hammond*, prior to docking at the Purfleet Quay and depositing his valuable prize at the Customs House in King's Lynn. He

[1] Captain Rogers had already demonstrated to local smugglers that he was a man of action and considerable courage. In June 1784, the *Speedy* was patrolling the North Norfolk coastline when two smuggling cutters were seen in the new harbour channel at Thornham. (See Faden's Map). The Captain launched three rowing boats carrying only thirty armed mariners; despite being heavily outnumbered by over one hundred variously armed smuggling sympathisers from Thornham village, the Captain won a violent skirmish in the harbour creek. In the process, he captured one of the smuggling cutters, seized 500 tubs of brandy, and put the villagers to flight. A detailed account of Rogers' four-year campaign against the smugglers of North Norfolk appears in a later chapter.
[2] It was normal practice for captains of Admiralty warships and Customs Cutters to employ the services of a supplementary vessel or tender. The *Lady Hammond* had been captured by Captain Rogers from a smuggler off Winterton, and he used the impressed vessel frequently in coastal creeks because of its shallow draft.
[3] Robert Forshaw was one of a large number of smugglers who lived around the Old Harbour at Oldfield Green, Thornham. Forshaw was not on board the *Revenge* at the time of its capture.

The Purfleet Quay, King's Lynn, late 18th century. A three-masted, 14-gun Royal Navy warship awaits the tide. Seven cannons protrude on the port side, with a similar number out of view on the starboard. HMS *Speedy*, commanded by Captain Rogers on North Sea smuggling duty, was of similar specification. At the extreme right of the painting is the Custom House.

was clearly well aware of the voracious drinking habits of his crew-men. At a later date, he would receive his half share of the financial proceeds of the subsequent auctioning of his captured goods. Also off-loaded at the port were the captured smugglers from the *Revenge*, where they were handed over to the appropriate authorities on charges of assisting in the illegal running of contraband goods.

Meanwhile, Captain Rogers' relentless search for Kemball continued. He boarded numerous vessels in North Norfolk waters, and in the process amassed huge profits in prize money. Although he made several mistakes, such as intercepting 'a sloop with an innocent cargo bound for Wisbech', a 'lobster smack off Brancaster' and a 'Burnham vessel carrying oats off Winterton', he continued nevertheless to seize large quantities of contraband from real smuggling vessels. His log records that he kept his crew vigilant and efficient by regular use of the lash for offences such as insubordination, slackness and drunkenness.

Rogers' persistence was rewarded finally, though not in the manner he would have wished. On the 15th April 1786, while the Captain was on shore leave in Great Yarmouth, the *Lady Hammond,* under the command of Rogers' lieutenant, sighted a smuggling schooner hovering to the north of Burnham Flats, some eight miles due north of Burnham Overy Staithe. In a written entry in his log dated 20th April, Captain Rogers took full credit for the three-hour northward sea chase that ensued and which culminated in the capture off the Yorkshire coast of both the smuggling vessel, named the *Fairy,* and its master, one William Kemball. In a letter to the Admiralty of the same date, Rogers wrote: 'Both the vessel and the cargo, consisting of 365 tubs of geneva, 198 tubs of cognac and a quantity of tea and tobacco, I have caused to be delivered to the Customs Collector at the port of Hull'. Confusingly he added: 'As I have received information that two warrants have been issued to apprehend Kemball for crimes committed by him on the west coast of England, I have put him in confinement, and ordered the necessary steps to be taken in order to bring him to justice'.

A NEW BEGINNING
1786-1793

Captain Rogers' letter is indeed confusing. He did not specify where he had confined Kemball, nor did he specify whether the confinement was civil or naval. Furthermore, while it was true that warrants for the arrest of Kemball for breaking the conditions of bail were in existence at the time of his arrest by Rogers' lieutenant, they were not, as Rogers claimed, for alleged criminal acts, and certainly not 'for crimes committed on the west coast of England'. All the documentary evidence suggests that Rogers did not deliver Kemball to the civil authorities because, when summoned to appear at the Exchequer Court a few weeks after his supposed confinement, Kemball failed to appear. In addition, if Kemball had been in civil confinement in April, why would Christopher Stangroom have written to his Supervisor in the Excise department in May requesting further arrest warrants 'in case of Kemball being detained'? Again, if Kemball had been handed over to the civil authorities, why were those who issued subsequent arrest warrants against Kemball, i.e. the Excise Department and the Attorney General, unaware, seemingly, of his arrest?

There can be no definitive answer to these questions, in the absence of conclusive documentary evidence, but in all likelihood, it was the Navy which detained Kemball, below the deck of the *Lady Hammond* and subsequently the *Speedy*. Thereafter, it is impossible to say what became of him. One strong possibility is that the Navy extended indefinitely its detention of Kemball, and effectively pressed him into service. By extensive use of their much feared Press Gangs, the Royal Navy was empowered to enlist unwilling victims forcibly, notably in the vicinity of ale-houses in ports and coastal towns. It was not unknown for the Press Gangs to enlist known smugglers; by enlisting Kemball, the Navy would have secured the services of a first rate sailor and navigator, whose skill in seamanship and whose knowledge of the French and English coasts might prove to be invaluable against the old enemy across the English Channel.

This possibility would account for Kemball's immediate disappearance and for his failure to appear at the Exchequer Courts in May and November of 1786, the latter of which proceedings confiscated all Kemball's goods and chattels, together with any freehold property in England, in lieu of the accumulated, but unpaid, fines. Gunton, incidentally, suffered similar forfeiture. In the long term, it is impossible to imagine that Kemball would have endured the indignity, enforced discipline and subservience below deck on a Royal Navy warship. As a natural leader of men, he would have gained immediately the admiration and support of his fellow mariners, many of whom would have been ex-smugglers and unwilling victims of the Navy's impress service. Sooner rather than later, they would have facilitated Kemball's escape, and he would have returned, not to his native Norfolk, but to the relative peace and security of Dunkirk in northern France. There he would be made welcome, not only by the large expatriate community of Englishmen who, as we have seen, based their business there, but by the French authorities who had good reason to regard Kemball and his associates with approval because of the social and economic damage their illicit trading had inflicted on the English government.

By contrast, England in general and Norfolk in particular were too dangerous and too hostile for Kemball to contemplate a return visit in the immediate future. If, as seems likely, he returned to Dunkirk towards the end of 1786, he would have faced not only strategic but also financial restraints on his immediate return to the business of smuggling. As a result of the capture and confiscation of his cutter the *Fairy* by the Royal Navy, together with its enormous cargo of contraband in April of that year, Kemball would have suffered unprecedented loss of his financial assets. In addition, his working capital had been depleted by his long and expensive legal battles from the time of his initial arrest for murder in September 1784 to the time of his release on bail from the Exchequer Court in April 1785. The latest loss of his biggest ever consignment of smuggled commodities, consisting of no less than 365 tubs of gin and 198 tubs of brandy, the sequestration of his English property and capital assets by the Exchequer Court, and the impounding of his vessel, the most valuable asset of all, would have left Kemball in dire financial straits. In simple terms, with no vessel and no capital with which to purchase his commodities, an immediate return to smuggling was out of the question.

Strategic obstacles to resuming his career on the beaches of Norfolk and elsewhere in England were also present on a massive scale. He was still being hunted by the Excise Board; he had murdered an Army dragoon and an Officer of Customs; he was clearly a prime target for the Royal Navy, whose vigorous patrolling of the coasts of England since returning from foreign conflict and commitment had severely compromised the activities of not only Kemball, but of all smuggling entrepreneurs. It is clear from Captain Rogers' relentless pursuit of Kemball that he was a marked man, and he must have realised that any attempt to resurrect his career in the foreseeable future was doomed to fail. Kemball may have been tempted to try his luck elsewhere on the coasts of England, where he was unknown, but it would not have been easy, or indeed prudent, to attempt to trespass on the territories of other smuggling barons, who were, to a man, extremely possessive and violently protective of their own landing beaches.

This limitation on Kemball's smuggling career remained in place for a further three years, until near the end of the decade. On 14th July, 1789, a momentous event in European history took place in Paris with the fall of the Bastille, which led eventually to the formation of the French Revolutionary Government and its declaration of war on Britain at the beginning of February 1793. A French invasion of Britain was a very real threat, leading to the rapid construction of defensive forts around the south and east coasts. It also led directly to the withdrawal of all Royal Navy vessels from smuggling duty, in order to concentrate on the defence of the realm and to engage in maritime warfare against the French on a global scale. It was effectively a green light to the smuggling barons to continue their operations in favourable conditions similar to those which existed in the early 1780s, when the Royal Navy was heavily engaged in the War of American Independence. The French Revolutionary Wars dragged on for over 20 years, up to the time of the Battle of Waterloo in 1815, and provided Kemball and his colleagues with the perfect opportunity to resurrect their careers. In addition, the Army's Dragoon and Foot Regiments were also withdrawn from the war against smuggling in order to confront the powerful French regiments on the battlefields of Europe. To make matters even more favourable to the smuggling fraternity, import taxes on tea, tobacco and spirits to pay for the escalating cost of the long war reached unprecedented levels, thus affording even greater profitability to illicit importation.

Kemball would have seized upon this fortuitous turn of historical events with the rapaciousness of a born opportunist. The eventual fate of Britain was not his concern; for him, the War represented a new and profitable beginning; it was business as usual.

EPILOGUE

Fate was not so kind to Peter Bullard, one of Kemball's landing-party on the beaches of Thornham and Old Hunstanton on the two nights before the murders of the Dragoon and the Customs Officer. In June 1785, nine months after the fateful shootings, Bullard was arrested, not for his part in the murders, but for stealing a brown mare, valued at £5, from Martin Greenacre at Ingoldisthorpe. He was found guilty at the Summer Assizes in Norwich the following month, and was sentenced to death. According to newspaper reports in the *Norfolk Chronicle* and the *Norwich Mercury*, Bullard behaved with great dignity as he was taken to the Castle ditches for execution. With echoes of the final words delivered by James Cliffen, the highway murderer from Yaxham, just a few months previously, Bullard addressed the spectators of his imminent departure from the world with a damning indictment of the smuggler William Kemball :-

'Kemball was not innocent. I was working the goods ashore for him on the night the officer and the soldier were killed. Kemball, in my presence, fired the first gun which killed the soldier. Then, with threats against our lives, he obliged us all to fire.'

Moments later, Bullard took the fatal drop, and was launched into eternity.

A Preventive Officer of either the Customs or the Excise, armed with a
pair of flint-lock pistols and a sword. In the 1780s, there was no official
uniform for officers of either service, although the baggy trousers and
belted jacket were standard apparel.

A Tale of Two Enemies:

Robert Bliss and Thomas Franklyn
North West Norfolk, 1779 to 1783.

During the four year period from 1779 to 1783, two men of contrasting ambitions battled for territorial supremacy along the North West Norfolk coastline, between the village of Old Hunstanton and the port of Wells next the Sea.

Robert Bliss, Excise Superintendent at the port of Wells, led the forces of law in a series of local clashes with a land-based smuggler from King's Lynn by the name of Thomas Franklyn.

The long running feud between two explosive personalities culminated in a violent encounter in Thornham village on 31st December, 1782.

The following pages describe in detail the inevitable collision, together with its causes and consequences.

Robert Bliss

A letter from the head-quarters of the Excise Board in London arrived at the office of the Winchester Excise district. It was addressed to Robert Bliss and was marked 'Private and Confidential'. Bliss read the contents with much satisfaction:-

> Robert Bliss Esquire,
> The Excise Office,
> Winchester,
> Hampshire.
> 30 March 1779
>
> In recognition of exemplary service over a period of ten years, the Board has pleasure in extending its invitation to the aforesaid Robert Bliss, Officer of Excise, to accept the position of Superintendent of Excise at the port of Wells juxta mare, Norfolk, at a salary of one hundred guineas per annum.

The offer of career advancement from head office was not unexpected. Bliss posted his acceptance immediately, relishing both the promotion and the prospect of working in a maritime district. Ambitious officers welcomed a posting to a district containing many miles of coastline; as Superintendent at Wells, Bliss would be responsible for confronting smugglers and seizing contraband from the beaches of Old Hunstanton, at the western extremity of the ride, to Stiffkey at the eastern end. Taking into account the recent upsurge in smuggling activity along that particular stretch of coast, Bliss anticipated opportunities for pocketing large rewards in prize money.

The Excise Board was confident that it had appointed the right man for a region as volatile as North Norfolk. Bliss was a single man, an important consideration in a job where commitment to duty, at all hours of the day and night, was a vital ingredient. In addition, Bliss, a physically powerful man of 32 years, had already proved himself to be unflinching in armed combat against the odds, by his refusal to be intimidated by gangs of aggressive smugglers. Such qualities would be severely tested in the troubled area in which he took up residence in May 1779. Whether or not his formidable reputation had preceded him to Norfolk is uncertain, but within days of arriving at the Excise Office in Wells, Bliss was the target of an anonymous and threatening letter, similar in content to one received by the Excise Superintendent at Diss. Written in a reasonably literate hand, it read:-

> BLISS. As you have begun to plunder and deprive us of our property, we will now begin with you and your followers for your blood. We are determined to have you or any that belong to you, by night or by day, sooner or later you plundering rascal. We can have two hundred men to join us any day we please. As such we bid you defiance and determined we are to have at you, for by God we will have your lives.
>
> These are from
>   'Free Englishmen'

Bliss was well aware of the popular belief amongst the smuggling community that Excise Officers, along with their colleagues in the Customs, represented the forces of tyranny and extortion and that their powers of search and entry had led to accusations of harassment, theft, trespass, rape and infringement of civil liberty. Bliss was also aware that the smugglers' self-styled title of 'Free Englishmen' was nothing more than a romanticised euphemism for marauding malcontents, whose only genuine grievance against the Excise was that its officers possessed both the legal power and the ability to seize smuggled goods wherever they were hidden, thereby reducing the profit margins of an illicit business. Some Officers of Excise had undeniably, on occasions, acted in an over-zealous manner in the execution of their statutory powers. On the other hand, smugglers had a well-earned reputation for extreme and sadistic violence. The *Norwich Mercury* had recently reported the fate of an Excise Officer in Essex, whose four limbs had been severed from his body, and the skin stripped from his face. The 'Free Englishmen' responsible for the outrage had tied to the unrecognisable human remains a piece of parchment, inscribed with the victim's name, for the purpose of identification.

Bliss put the letter to one side on his desk with a dismissive gesture, and turned his attention to more important matters. He had called a meeting in his office near the quay in order to make acquaintance with his new subordinate colleagues. There were three Excise Officers under his command; of these, William Spencer had five years' experience in the Wells area, while Thomas Abbott and John Banham were relative newcomers. Spencer was particularly useful in providing Bliss with the names of high-ranking smugglers in his new district, together with information regarding the beaches and creeks most favoured for the landing of contraband goods. Two names were prominent in Spencer's briefing; both from King's Lynn, Thomas Franklyn and William Kemball were co-owners of an impressive smuggling lugger and partners in a well organised business. Spencer expressed a grudging admiration for Kemball, whom he described as an expert sailor, rarely seen on land. Thomas Franklyn, on the other hand, was essentially a land-based smuggler for whom, it was rumoured, even the shortest journey afloat was an ordeal likely to cause violent sickness. He was the distributor of the goods landed by his partner and was responsible for leading and directing large gangs of carriers and teams of pack-horses on the first stage of an intricate relay system which led, eventually, to London. At the same time, Franklyn could not resist the temptation of profiteering locally, and supplied on a regular basis most of the innkeepers and wealthier inhabitants of the maritime villages within easy reach of his favourite landing beaches at Old Hunstanton, Holme and Thornham. Franklyn was an enormously popular figure in these and other neighbouring villages, from all of which he claimed to have the active support of up to two hundred men, to help land smuggled goods on the beaches, transport them inland, and act as an armed protection mob when necessary. He recruited his 'troops' in the village inns and alehouses, notably the Cutter at Old Hunstanton, the White Horse at Holme, and the King's Head, Red Cow and Chequers at Thornham. These shabby hostelries, according to Spencer, witnessed regular pay-days, when cash payments were distributed to grateful members of Franklyn's private armies, for services rendered, in scenes of riotous conviviality.

Robert Bliss listened with great interest as his experienced colleague assessed and outlined the problems likely to be encountered by any projected attempt to confront the local smuggling malaise. Spencer advised his new supervisor that, although considerable sums in prize-money were to be made in the small stretch of coastline he had just described, there would be violent opposition from Franklyn and his primitive village armies. He warned against any attempts to enter these utterly lawless villages unless accompanied and supported by a large detachment of cavalry soldiers from a dragoon regiment. The current War in America had necessitated the withdrawal of many home-based regiments from coastal duty, so that military support was not always obtainable or even available. At this time, one troop on detachment from the 2nd Regiment of Dragoons was billeted at Holt, a small market town about five miles inland. Spencer recommended a meeting with the troop's Captain, to determine how much man-power was available. As a final piece of advice, Spencer warned against seeking help from the local part-time soldiers who were compulsorily recruited to the ranks of the Norfolk Militia. They were amateurs, chosen at random by ballot from the youth of the county, and were intended to supplement the Army when regular forces were called abroad. Employing these recruits in raids against smugglers should be avoided in all circumstances. Not only were they ill-disciplined and untrustworthy, but were also likely, in mid-battle, to take side with the smuggling gangs, of which many were members.

Bliss was grateful for all Spencer's information; it had been a most productive briefing. His next task was to journey to Holt, where he had requested a meeting at the Feathers Inn with the Captain of the troop of dragoons billeted in the town, on detachment from the Regiment's temporary headquarters in Norwich. Bliss requested the transfer to Wells of the Captain's entire troop of 33 officers and men, to provide instantly available forces for large-scale raids against smugglers along the coast. The Dragoon Captain refused the request, claiming that his Colonel's Regiment was essentially a heavy cavalry force, employing sturdy and slow-moving horses, better suited to suppressing town riots than to chasing smugglers over rough countryside and muddy creeks at night. In his opinion, a Light Dragoon Regiment, which was a faster and more nimble cavalry force, would be more appropriate for the task. The suggestion might have been a sensible one, had there been such a regiment closer to hand than at Bury St Edmunds in the neighbouring county of Suffolk. Bliss realised at once that he was dealing with extreme incompetence and that the young Captain was, regrettably, of a type of cavalry officer to be found in abundance in the British Army. Of limited experience and intelligence, he had purchased, but certainly not earned, his initial commission as an ensign with the help of family money and connections. His subsequent promotion to the rank of Captain was similarly achieved; no doubt further promotions via the same route of patronage would follow. In effect, he was an amateur in professional costume, adorned with an extravagantly expensive uniform of exotic colour and exquisite taste, who regarded his Army commission as a stepping stone to social grace, favour and opportunity. Bliss strongly suspected that the Captain's reason for remaining with his troop in Holt had nothing to do with the relative merits of heavy or light dragoon cavalry. Holt was an attractive and pleasant town, and popular with the local gentry; accommodation at the Feathers Inn was warm, comfortable and of a standard befitting an officer of the 2nd Regiment of Dragoons. By contrast, Wells was a damp and dismal town, especially when the north wind raged over the sea. It was noisy and unrelaxing, and the smell of rotting fish permeated its mean and narrow streets. Above all, it was the haunt of common sailors of all nationalities, and fishermen.

Bliss rode back to Wells in a mood of anger and frustration following his unproductive meeting with the Dragoon Captain. It was a difficult time for him; as a new-comer to a position of considerable responsibility, he was understandably anxious to confront the smuggling problem directly and expeditiously, at the head of an armed force capable of overpowering a well-organised opposition. In the short time that he had been Superintendent of Excise, reports of unopposed landings of contraband goods along his stretch of coastline had arrived almost daily. Without military support, he was powerless to act. Back in his office at Wells, he wrote the first of many letters to the Secretary of State at the War Office headquarters in London, requesting a military presence in his newly adopted port, at the same time emphasising the impossibility of his appointed task to control the smuggling epidemic, unless properly equipped with military man-power. Replies to his letters, throughout the year 1779, repeated over and again the same message, that troops were in short supply owing to the War in America, and that such regiments as were available had been sent to the coasts of Kent and Sussex, which were completely over-run by smuggling gangs. At the present time, no further troops could be spared for coastal duty in Norfolk.

The innkeepers of Wells paid the immediate price of Bliss's suppressed ambitions. In common with · the majority of licensees throughout the country, the publicans of Wells practised a system of purchasing small quantities of a variety of spirits, such as brandy, rum and gin, legally and with duty fully paid, to give the appearance of legitimate stock. For every gallon so purchased, a further fifty or more would be supplied by the smuggling gangs, illegally and with duty unpaid. Acting upon information that smuggled Dutch gin had been distributed recently to the port's inns and taverns, Bliss gathered all his employees, including officers, tide-waiters, boatmen and porters in readiness for simultaneous raids on six licensed establishments. Twenty-five gallons of spirits were seized at the quay-side Fleece Inn, with a further fifteen gallons at the Red Lion; smaller quantities were confiscated at the Standard, the Tuns, the Bowling Green and the Fighting Cocks.

The Excise operation in Wells was significant more for marking the beginning of Bliss's activities in North Norfolk than for the size of the seizure. A mere one hundred gallons of Geneva, confiscated from the six taverns, was a disappointingly small return from an action which bred instant hostility and resentment in the immediate neighbourhood. Bliss was unconcerned; he had come to Norfolk to accumulate prize-money, not to gain friends. He persisted with requests to the War Office for military support and was rewarded for his efforts, at the beginning of 1780, when the 1st Regiment of Dragoons was despatched to Norwich with specific instructions 'to assist the Officers of the Revenue against smugglers and smuggling'. The port of Wells continued to be denied its own resident complement of dragoons; nevertheless, detachments of the Regiment were billeted strategically at Fakenham, Holt, Walsingham and Burnham Market[1], each commanded by a Lieutenant or Captain with orders to engage the 'participants in illegal importation'.

It was the moment Bliss had eagerly awaited; not surprisingly, he took full and immediate advantage of the new and improved opportunity. Throughout the early months of 1780, he led frequent expeditions to the hostile coastal villages in 'Franklyn territory', supported always by a fully-armed raiding-party of twelve Dragoons, together with his own Excise Officers. Old Hunstanton was regularly targeted; huge quantities of contraband were seized from a variety of hiding places in the village and were carried back to the Excise Office in Wells. There is no evidence to suggest that Bliss was seriously opposed by smuggling gangs, a state of affairs which, happily for him, continued throughout the years 1780, 1781 and 1782. Some seizures produced spectacular results. On 5th February 1780, no less than one thousand gallons of gin, together with 400 pounds of tea and 200 pounds of camphor, were confiscated in one night raid in Old Hunstanton. Five hundred gallons of brandy, rum and Geneva were discovered under a vault in a farmyard hog-sty at Ringstead in November 1781, while a massive twelve hundred gallons of various liquors were successfully rescued from a barn at the Red Cow alehouse in Thornham in January 1782. Auction sales of seized contraband goods became a regular feature of Wells life during these productive years, and the personal coffers of Bliss, his Excise colleagues and the Dragoon Officers associated with the successful raids swelled immeasurably. Bliss used the Thornham seizure to impress upon the War Office the urgent need to guard the Excise warehouse at Wells, currently full to capacity with in excess of three thousand gallons of spirits, with a resident military force. In a letter dated 25 January 1782 to the Secretary of State for War, Bliss explained that local smugglers were so exasperated by his successful exploits that plans were afoot to storm the poorly protected building. The War Office acted immediately, allocating six dragoons from the 19th Regiment to Wells, with specific instructions to safeguard

---

[1] Dragoons of the 1st Regiment were billeted as follows:-
    Fakenham: The Crown and The Red Lion
    Burnham Market: The Pitt Arms
    Holt: The Feathers, The Lion, The King's Head and The Dolphin

the warehouse contents: from then until the end of the decade, the port of Wells was provided with a regular, resident military detachment, dedicated to smuggling prevention duty.

With the support of a succession of Dragoon Regiments placed at his disposal and locally billeted, Bliss was able to raid the villages of Burnham Norton, Burnham Deepdale, Brancaster, Thornham, Old Hunstanton, Ringstead and Holme almost at will. Up to the end of 1782, Bliss had good reason to be satisfied with the financial rewards of his mainly successful activities. In each of three consecutive years, he had seen his annual salary boosted ten-fold by his share of the proceeds from confiscated goods auctioned monthly on the quay-side at Wells.[1]

The seizure of a large quantity of tea and spirits, discovered in the tower of Old Hunstanton Church on Christmas Eve 1782, proved to be Bliss's last successful operation. The reputation and finances of Thomas Franklyn had suffered acutely since Bliss first undertook regular armed incursions into the smuggler's territory. Franklyn had to take a stand against Bliss, or risk losing both his credibility and his business empire. Almost the entire population of Old Hunstanton village had been present at the church, when Bliss emptied the tower of Franklyn's goods during the Yule-tide service.[2] It was imperative that Franklyn should act, and quickly; within just seven days of the latest indignity, he took his revenge.

---

[1] Bliss was not the only Government agent active in the area at this time. The Excise Superintendent at King's Lynn, together with the Customs Riding Officers attached to both Wells and King's Lynn, were also making their own regular seizures along the same stretch of coastline between the two ports. If the calculation is correct, that for every gallon of spirits seized by the authorities, a further one hundred gallons slipped through the Preventive Service net, then illegal landings of contraband on the beaches of North West Norfolk at this time were indeed on a massive scale.

[2] It is not known whether the Vicar of Old Hunstanton, the Reverend Bird, was aware that his church tower was being used as a temporary hiding place for smuggled goods. Suffice it to say, that his contemporary, the Reverend James Woodforde, rector of Weston Longville, was by his own admission a regular receiver and consumer of contraband goods between the years 1777 and 1789.

THOMAS FRANKLYN

By the time Bliss arrived on promotion at the Excise Office in Wells in 1779, Thomas Franklyn had already established his own authority along the coastline of North West Norfolk. As we have seen, he was the co-owner of a smuggling lugger named *The Lively*, in partnership with William Kemball. Both men were born and raised in King's Lynn, were of similar ages and had been acquaintances since childhood, nurturing a shared fascination for sailing vessels, their cargoes, and ultimately, the potential profits to be gained from smuggling. They acquired at an early age the attributes of mental agility and physical aggression, characteristics which would serve them well in the unscrupulous society into which they were born. There was one major difference between the two personalities. While Kemball loved sails, masts, waves, tides, navigation and all the paraphernalia associated with sailing, and was in his partner's opinion the best sailing master in the smuggling business, Franklyn was happy only on land.

Unlike his business partner, Franklyn was born into poverty and squalor in King's Lynn's north end; he received no education and was illiterate even as an adult, unable to write his own name.[1] His first employment was as a labourer in the warehouse of a King's Lynn fell-monger, who traded in animal skins imported from America and the Arctic. At the same time, he became involved with the smuggling trade, undertaking deliveries of small quantities of smuggled tea to households in King's Lynn, in order to supplement his modest wages. From such small beginnings was to blossom an extensive distribution network under his personal control. A gift for organisational detail allied to an intimidating physical presence guaranteed Franklyn a meteoric rise to capitalist status. At the peak of his career in the early 1780s, he employed hundreds of part-time carriers recruited in the villages of north-west Norfolk. He claimed to have on his pay-roll the names of two hundred men in each of the three coastal villages of Old Hunstanton, Holme and Thornham; in practice, although support on such a scale would have

---

[1] An entry in the Parish Register of St. Nicholas Church, King's Lynn, records the marriage in 1777 of Franklyn's brother John to Mary Holman. As chief witness to the ceremony, Franklyn was required to counter-sign the entry; he was able only to inscribe his mark in the form of an 'x'.

A land-based smuggler awaiting a landing of contraband on a beach, armed with a pair of flint-lock pistols, a sword, and wearing leather wading boots. Thomas Franklyn was one of many such smuggling barons in the 1780s.

involved almost every able-bodied male from the labouring classes in each village, it was not an idle boast. The inhabitants of this remote coastal region were ripe for recruitment to a business which provided good wages, which in turn bought food for hungry mouths. Social discontent in the area had been simmering for decades as economic impoverishment beckoned. Although the enclosures of the open fields and common lands had not yet been authorised officially by Parliament, the process of gradual erosion of small-holdings had left the rural population bereft of arable land, grazing meadows and commons rights. With the exception of a few landowners, most of the population had become landless labourers, dependent entirely upon their masters who provided employment only when it suited them, and at a wage which was not negotiable. Financially, they were less secure than their forefathers had been under the feudal system of medieval times.

Thomas Franklyn was not concerned unduly about the impoverished circumstances of the agrarian population living conveniently close to his favourite landing beaches. He was simply an opportunist who took full advantage of the distress and was able to recruit a readily available and ever-willing private army to land, hide, protect and transport the increasing quantities of smuggled goods imported by his partner. At the height of Kemball and Franklyn's activities in the early 1780s, an average of two thousand gallons of Geneva, rum and brandy, together with one thousand pounds weight of tea, were being landed weekly on the mainly unguarded beaches between Old Hunstanton and the west harbour at Thornham. Smuggling on such a scale provided one night's work each week for most of Franklyn's supporters from the villages; in addition, the stronger members of his local army were engaged a further two nights each week, lending their muscles to the Herculean task of transporting the contraband on the long trek inland.

The significant feature of the employment provided by Franklyn and by others of his kind, around the entire coast-line of England, was the high rate of financial remuneration earned by the labouring classes. As a general rule, one night's work in the employment of a smuggling baron was equivalent, in terms of wages, to a whole week's labour on the land for the local squire. Those labourers who worked as full-time retainers in the smuggling business earned unprecedented cash rewards. Not surprisingly, landowners in maritime districts bemoaned the disastrous effects of large-scale smuggling activity in their area. During the busier months of the agricultural calendar, such as harvest-time, labourers were reluctant to work on the land. Those who were recruited by the landowners either demanded greatly increased wages, or were the old and infirm, overlooked by the likes of Franklyn. With more than a touch of hypocrisy, landowners complained to their Members of Parliament about the resulting diminution of their levels of profit; at the same time, they readily purchased cut-price brandy, tea, silk and other luxury goods from the same entrepreneurs whose businesses they attempted to curtail, and about whom they vociferously complained.

Franklyn and Kemball organised and supervised every stage of their complicated business of running contraband. Kemball, as we have seen, purchased whatever goods commanded high English import duties from wholesalers in Dunkirk or Flushing. The cargo was then carried aboard his vessel, the spirits and liquors contained in small wooden casks of manageable weight, and perishables such as tea in water-resistant, oil-skin bags. These initial stages were relatively simple, conducted with the blessing and connivance of the French and Dutch authorities who regarded English smugglers as unwitting allies, instrumental in no small way in undermining the economic and social fabric of the rival state across the Channel. By contrast, the third stage was hazardous in the extreme, and involved steering a course between the European mainland and the Norfolk coast, avoiding the hostile attention of English naval warships, English Customs cutters and, most unpredictable of all, omnivorous pirate vessels, the stateless piranhas of the oceans, who fed off any vessel that sailed the seven seas. Given the frequency of Kemball's nautical journeys during the years of his supremacy afloat, it says much for his skilful seamanship, his cunning and his adroit distribution of bribes, that he was apprehended at sea with a full cargo on only two occasions.

The fourth stage of the operation was potentially the most dangerous and difficult of all; landing the contraband on Norfolk beaches was a combined operation which involved Kemball at sea and Franklyn on land, and which demanded precise and highly-tuned planning. In the absence of any form of long distance communications, Kemball's time, or even date, of arrival at any given stretch of Norfolk coastline would have been, at best, an approximation. Weather conditions were impossible to forecast, in particular the strength and direction of the winds upon which the speed and mobility of all ocean-going vessels were dependant. Regardless of the difficulties, it was imperative that contact be made between the smugglers afloat and their comrades ashore as soon as the heavily-laden smuggling lugger entered local Norfolk waters, in order to set in motion a series of complicated preparations for landing the cargo. Sufficient numbers of men, horses, carts and landing equipment had to be made available on a specific beach at the appropriate time. Precise synchronisation of every manoeuvre was vital. All elements of the landing operation had to be in place simultaneously to beach the contraband successfully, transport it to the nearest village and secrete it in secure hiding places in the shortest possible time without attracting the attentions of the authorities on land or at sea.

A variety of means of signalling or passing information from sea to shore, including exploding flares and carrier pigeons, was employed by smugglers around the entire coastline of England. Franklyn's preferred method was to despatch members of his private army to strategic points some miles to the east of the intended landing beaches. His 'lookouts', equipped with telescopes and light, nimble horses, would ride to suitable lookout areas, such as the elevated ground behind Stiffkey village, and wait patiently, sometimes for a period of forty-eight hours, alternating the watch at regular intervals, until a pre-arranged signal in the form of a gunpowder flare had been fired from Kemball's west-bound lugger afloat. The watch-men would then ride to Thornham at full gallop, usually to the King's Head alehouse, to provide the resident Franklyn with an estimated time of arrival of Kemball's cargo. Immediately, messengers would be despatched from the alehouse to ride around the village, knocking on doors, raising the landing army, and giving instructions as to when and where to assemble. Columns of horses, mules, carts, wagons and primitively armed villagers, carrying pistols and cudgels, would converge on the appointed stretch of shore-line, usually to the west of the new harbour channel, via numerous marshy tracks and temporary creek-bridges known only to the local population. Simultaneously, Franklyn would send further messengers to neighbouring Holme to alert the resident army in the village to be ready to receive the second portion of Kemball's cargo. It was too time-consuming, and therefore too risky, to land an entire cargo on one beach; on occasions, as many as six different landing places would be chosen, with the final part of the consignment being beached on the Lincolnshire coast on the far side of The Wash.

The transfer of the cargo, from lugger afloat to the landing armies on the beaches, was potentially the most hazardous part of the operation, because of the vulnerability of the participants to attack from various government forces, both at sea and on land. Once the all-clear signal, in the form of a flaming torch, had been raised by Franklyn or one of his lieutenants, there would follow a period of concentrated and breathless activity, as heavily-laden, oar-powered long boats brought the bulky consignment to the shore. The landings were often conducted at night, in winter, at times in freezing conditions; it was a task for men of great mental courage and even greater muscular strength. The physical task of beaching the immensely heavy rowing boats, of lifting pairs of rope-slung barrels over the shoulders of the tub-carriers, and of loading the teams of mules and pack-horses with bulging oil-skin bags, in the quickest possible time, with hands and fingers numbed by the bone-chilling wind and water, was of a severity to defy the imagination.

The tub-carriers, known as 'tubmen', were the elite of Franklyn's village army, and amongst the highest paid. Hired for their strength, the tubmen were required to carry two kegs, one on the chest and one on the back, a load of approximately six stones in weight, at a brisk pace and over unsympathetic terrain, such as sand-dunes, marshes and slippery muddy tracks.[1] Proceeding from the beach, the tubmen's first duty was to carry their allocation to the security of temporary hiding-places in the nearest coastal village. They were accompanied on the journey by teams of pack-horses and mules, led by the reins and laden with bags of tea and silk; for protection, the entire convoy was flanked by another specialist group from the village, known as 'batmen'. Apart from brandishing the long wooden clubs from which they took their name, they were additionally armed with pistols and sabres, and were recruited by Franklyn for their aggression and powers of intimidation. Some batmen brought with them, snarling at the leash, their own specially trained and ferocious dogs, whose presence in the convoy contributed an extra and even sinister element of terror to an overwhelmingly aggressive spectacle. Moving in a tight and closely-knit formation, protected, armed, organised and resolute, the private army of coastal guerrillas, marching

---

[1] The working lives of tubmen were often curtailed by severe spinal damage as a direct result of their labours. Many succumbed to premature aging and even physical deformity; consequently, the sight of hunched and arthritic middle-aged men was commonplace in coastal villages in late 18th century England.

in great numbers, was virtually unassailable.

Curious places were chosen for the temporary concealment of contraband in coastal villages, a stage of the overall smuggling operation which attracted the attentions of Government forces more than any other. In common with other distributors around the coast of England, Franklyn had access, in his local villages of Thornham, Holme, Ringstead, Old Hunstanton and Heacham, to numerous agricultural barns, out-houses, hayricks, pig-sties, cattle sheds, windmills, cellars of ale-houses and domestic buildings, churchyard burial vaults, church towers and vestries. The final stages of Franklyn's operation, transporting the consignment inland and selling it to a dealer, took place as soon as possible after the beach landings and temporary village concealment. Storing large quantities of illegally imported goods for any length of time in the coastal villages was considered too risky because of the frequency of Customs or Excise raiding excursions. Preferably, their removal inland commenced at dusk the following evening, and involved transporting almost the entire consignment, leaving behind only small quantities to satisfy the demands and needs of local ale-house keepers, the wealthier gentry, and the clergy.

The route inland most favoured by Franklyn was the Peddars Way, an ancient track of Roman or even earlier origin, although other highways and byways were used to avoid predictability. From Franklyn's point of view, the Peddars Way was ideal in many ways, providing not only a direct link between the Norfolk coast and his customers some forty miles inland, but also a relatively fast and firm surface for his pack-horses, mules, carts and tubmen. Even in winter, the broad and grassy track was mainly dry underfoot, on account of its chalky subsoil. Furthermore, its course was direct, bypassing towns and, with a few exceptions, even small villages. The various village armies would assemble at Ringstead, near the northern end of the track, complete with all the contraband unloaded on the local beaches the previous night. The long night march inland of approximately forty miles, to a rendezvous with a dealer somewhere to the east of Thetford, close to the Suffolk border, was a joint operation, involving Franklyn's armed hordes from all his local villages. In all, between two and three hundred of his best village troops, chiefly batmen and tubmen, joined forces to form one enormous convoy even more intimidating than those that gathered on the landing beaches. From the moment the booty-laden column of carts,

A pursued smuggler opens fire on a sabre-wielding light dragoon.

Packhorses being loaded with barrels, wooden chests and oil-skin bags of contraband. The long trek inland, often involving over 200 armed smugglers, and a convoy of 100 wagons and horses, usually began at Ringstead and followed the course of the Peddars Way.

wagons, horses, out-riders, carriers and weapon-brandishing protection mob proceeded uncompromisingly inland, a clear and uninterrupted passage was assured. As the convoy rumbled through the occasional village en route in the middle of the night, as at Castle Acre some twenty miles inland, the local inhabitants hid behind closed doors, shutters and curtains. No-one dared to look and watch, for fear of being accused of spying. No-one resisted the occasional act of plunder perpetrated by the batmen, for fear of terrible retribution. No-one would intervene, least of all Customs or Excise Officers patrolling with a small party of cavalry. It would have required two or three entire troops of dragoons even to contemplate a confrontation. No army officer was ever prepared to chance such a manoeuvre; the loss of, and damage to, both horses and men would have been too great. In any case, the Army was reluctant to engage an essentially non-political and civilian opponent whilst on 'home duty', on such a scale, unless specifically instructed by the War Office. Nevertheless, this was the stage of the smuggling operation where the distributor barons such as Franklyn had most to lose, in the form of an entire cargo of immense value. It was therefore imperative to protect it with the full complement of forces at their disposal. This they did, and with enormous success. Indeed, in some areas of England, such as the south-eastern counties of Sussex and Kent, the private armies were so large and well armed, sometimes numbering up to seven hundred men, that the convoys of contraband were moved confidently, from Channel coast to London, in full daylight, and were similarly unhindered.

Once Franklyn's consignment of smuggled goods had reached the Suffolk border, it was transferred immediately to the waiting hands of the inland dealers, who themselves possessed armies of batmen and tubmen, together with the necessary transport. Franklyn, it appears, sold his contraband mainly to dealers from London, although on occasions it found its way to the cities of Cambridge and Norwich. The London armies were an especially fearful mob, recruited from the criminal infested rookeries and ghettoes of the Seven Dials district of Holborn. The batmen who worked for these gangs were an utterly lawless band of cut-throats who, in addition to providing protection for smuggling dealers, indulged in highway robbery and urban extortion.

It now remained for Franklyn to complete the chain of events which had begun some two weeks previously with the purchase of the merchandise in Dunkirk by his partner Kemball. Negotiation and hard bargaining with the London dealers was conducted in great secrecy, behind locked doors in a tavern room in the vicinity of the hand-over of the goods. Franklyn's numerate clerk was always present at this final stage, to ensure that the calculations were correct, and that the only acceptable currency of the smuggling trade, hard cash, was paid in full.

Following the financial settlement, Franklyn would ride back to the Norfolk coast, his horse, and those ridden by his supporters, heavily laden with the cash rewards of another successful mission. It was the easiest part of the whole operation, and probably the most satisfying. The rest of his army would follow, mainly on foot, leading the unburdened pack-horses and empty wagons back along the same route it had followed the previous night. For the tubmen in particular, a few days relaxation in their coastal villages, and an opportunity to rest aching muscles and tired limbs, before their next engagement, would be eagerly anticipated. As an additional bonus, each village that had participated in the beach landings and the transportation inland would stage a 'pay-night', when all members of the local armies, including carriers, protection mob, out-riders, lookouts, signalmen and messengers, would receive their wages, in proportion to their contribution to the overall operation. At the King's Head in Thornham, the White Horse in Holme and the Wheatsheaf in Heacham, Franklyn personally supervised the pay-off, employing the services of his literate clerk to allocate the relevant sums of cash to each employee. The rest of the evening would take its inevitable course; unlimited supplies of cheap spirits and liquors ensured that sobriety would be notably absent at the ensuing riotous celebrations.

Franklyn had established his personal control over the larger scale smuggling operations in North-west Norfolk by the year 1779, a year in which his success and profits reached their peak. The arrival of Robert Bliss at the Excise Office in Wells in the same year did not immediately affect the smuggler's supremacy. However, as the months passed, Bliss began to exert his influence. With the help of various Dragoon Regiments, whose local presence he persistently requested, a series of armed incursions into Franklyn's territory began to produce spectacular rewards. As we have seen in the previous chapter, major seizures of spirits, sometimes exceeding one thousand gallons in a single raid, during the years 1780, 1781 and 1782, in the heartland of Franklyn's territory, gave the smuggler serious cause for alarm. All the raids led by Bliss occurred during the smuggling stage of temporary village concealment, immediately after the beach landings. It was a policy he continued to pursue with increasing confidence, vigour and success. By the year 1782, Franklyn was losing unsustainable quantities of goods and profits, not only to Bliss's Excise raids, but also to those of the Excise Superintendent at King's Lynn.

The tide of fortune had clearly turned. Pressure was mounting on Franklyn from within his own organisation, notably from Kemball, who was becoming increasingly impatient with the frequent losses incurred by his land-based business partner. There were also murmurings of discontent from his once loyal village armies, who had seen their earnings and living standards decline as a direct result of the seizures affected by Bliss and his colleagues. Franklyn's reaction was predictable; he determined to meet the threat to his livelihood by confrontation, in the hope that intimidation and counter-attack might weaken the resolve of his enemies in general, and of Bliss in particular. Franklyn was no stranger to such tactics. During the month of July 1781, in his native King's Lynn, he assaulted and seriously injured three Customs employees, William Slater, Thomas Huggins and John Burch, in separate incidents in the vicinity of the port. The assaults on the three men, prompted by their attempts to seize smuggled tea, were exceptionally severe. When Franklyn appeared at the Quarter Sessions held at the Guildhall for the attack on Slater, he was charged with 'beating, assaulting, wounding and ill-treating' his adversary 'so that his life was greatly despaired of'. The physical attacks upon Huggins and Burch were similarly brutal. The derisory fines imposed upon Franklyn, of one shilling for each offence, were scarcely designed to deter him from future excesses against members of the preventive service. On the contrary, at the Quarter Sessions in October 1782, he was convicted of assault against the person of Thomas Gibson, another Customs Officer at the port of Lynn; he was fined six pence.[1] A few weeks later, in December 1782, in the village of Old Hunstanton, Franklyn threatened with assault and put to flight William Turner, the Excise Superintendent from King's

---

[1] It is tempting to suspect that the indulgence shown by Magistrates at the King's Lynn Quarter Sessions, in Franklyn's favour, was prompted by William Kemball senior, a minor court official at the Guildhall, and father of Franklyn's business partner. However, as we have seen earlier, courts of law were outrageously reluctant to punish local smugglers for even the most serious offences.

Lynn, who had shown great courage in seizing single-handedly a quantity of roasted coffee from two of Franklyn's local henchmen, Philip Summers and Charles Bunkey.

If Franklyn hoped, by such methods, to intimidate the formidable Robert Bliss, and to deter him from further armed raids in the maritime villages, he was much mistaken. Bliss was, without doubt, the most accomplished preventive officer on the Norfolk coast; the timing of his military-backed incursions into Franklyn's territory was particularly adroit, and it must be assumed that he had on his unofficial pay-roll a number of well-informed spies who were also prominent members of the village armies. The raid on Old Hunstanton village, on Christmas Eve, 1782, was typical of Bliss's strategy, in its planning, timing and execution. There had been major landings of brandy, gin and tea on the beaches of Old Hunstanton and Heacham on the night of 22 December, a significant proportion of which had been hidden temporarily in the lower section of the west tower of St Mary's Church in Old Hunstanton, for transportation inland on Christmas night. On receiving such intelligence from one of his informers, Bliss decided to surround and attack the church on Christmas Eve, during the Yuletide service. He knew that the entire village population, including many members of Franklyn's army, would be present in church to witness the humiliation of his adversary and the further damage to his diminishing reputation. More importantly, he calculated that, in the presence of the entire Le Strange family, one member of which was a permanent fixture on the County Assizes Grand Jury, and of at least two local Justices of the Peace, the Vicar and other influential gentry, he would not be opposed by Franklyn and his supporters, and would be guaranteed a free hand once inside the church.

The early evening service had begun; in the nave, the full congregation stood to sing a traditional advent carol, led by an enthusiastic choir-master and the heavy tone of the church organ. Outside the church, a column of cavalry belonging to the 11th Regiment of Light Dragoons, billeted at Wells and consisting of one sergeant and ten private soldiers, led by Robert Bliss and two of his Excise Officers, dismounted their horses in the churchyard. Bliss himself rode into the south porch, the hooves of his horse clattering cacophonously on the stone floor, as the full voice of the congregation sang of the advent of the new Messiah. Bliss lifted the latch of the south door and strode directly across the nave, at the head of his armed party of soldiers and subordinates. He reached the door leading to the west tower and beckoned two dragoons carrying lanterns to lead the way up the dark, stone, spiral staircase. The Vicar in his pulpit, acutely embarrassed that his patron and benefactor, and his wealthier parishioners, should witness such unseemly events, attempted to appear oblivious to the military interruption. Members of the congregation turned their heads in unison to the rear of the nave, and watched as a seemingly inexhaustible quantity of wooden barrels and oil-skin bags were passed through the tower doorway and across the nave, from dragoon to dragoon, to wagons requisitioned from farmer Clare and positioned in the lane outside the churchyard perimeter wall. Further concealed goods were removed from the base of the tower through the external doorway giving direct access to the churchyard.

The large seizure, which was stored in a safe house in the village overnight and transported to Wells Excise office on Christmas Day, marked yet another triumph for Bliss over his rival. Franklyn, who was present in the church during the removal of his smuggled goods, but was powerless to intervene, had now reached a point of crisis in his career. Kemball had already threatened to replace him with a more reliable partner if the serious losses continued, and more members of the village armies would desert their former master following the most recent disastrous events at Old Hunstanton. Franklyn returned to his lodgings at the King's Head in Thornham, where resided the nucleus of his most loyal supporters, to plan the rebuilding of his crumbling empire and the re-establishment of his territorial supremacy over the Excise Super-intendent from Wells. In the company of his two henchmen, Bunkey and Summers, an elaborate plot was devised, to lure Bliss into a one-sided physical confrontation with Franklyn's army in Thornham village. Within days of its conception, the plot unfolded in circumstances both dramatic and bloody.

VIOLENT ENCOUNTER IN THORNHAM VILLAGE

Robert Bliss was in a contented and benevolent mood as he dined with three Officers of the 11th Regiment of Light Dragoons at the Green Dragon in Wells, on the 26th December 1782. An enormous fire-place,

117

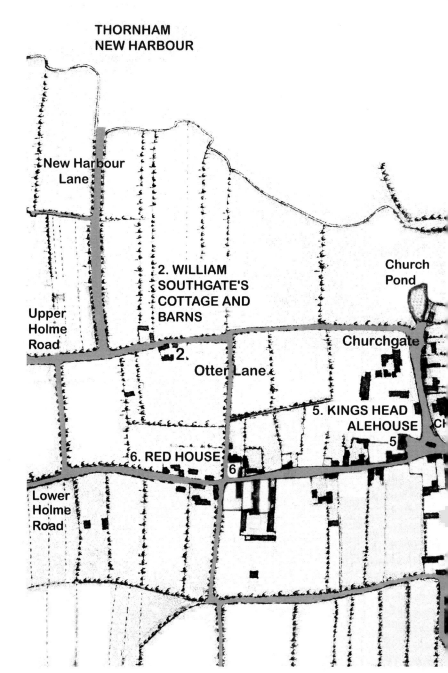

Thornham Village Centre, adapted from a Thornham Estate map of 1787, showing alehouses, cottages and lanes mentioned in the text.

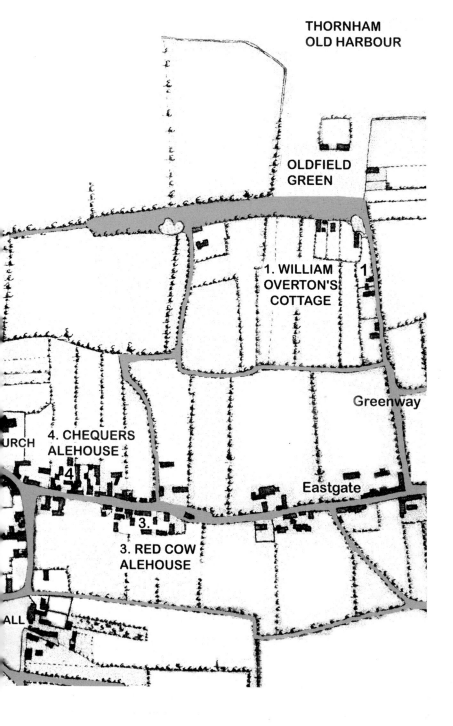

THORNHAM
OLD HARBOUR

OLDFIELD
GREEN

1. WILLIAM
OVERTON'S
COTTAGE

1

Greenway

4. CHEQUERS
ALEHOUSE

URCH

4

Eastgate

3.

3. RED COW
ALEHOUSE

ALL

generously stocked with burning logs, illuminated the dining-room with a warm, flickering glow; outside, a combination of rain and hail-stones lashed violently against the small leaded panes of window glass. The harbour was deserted, apart from the fishing smacks which bobbed and swayed in safe anchorage, riding the heavy swell. All human activity had ceased, as mariners and fishermen alike confined themselves to the security of the quayside alehouses. Bliss was enjoying the atmosphere and the splendid dinner, a magnificent sirloin of roast beef, followed by plum pudding and mince pies. He had missed the traditional festivities of Christmas Day, on account of his successful exploits at Old Hunstanton, but was determined to enjoy an evening of rare relaxation, away from the pressures and dangers of duty in the front line. The claret and French brandies were of exceptional quality; nevertheless, Bliss could not refrain from casting suspicious glances, firstly at the cut glass decanters and their intoxicating contents, then in the direction of the landlord, Mr Robert Sayer, who without doubt had purchased the evening's alcoholic offerings from an illicit source. Mr Sayer, acutely aware of the accusatory looks, studiously avoided direct eye-contact with the Exciseman; instead he shuffled nervously and attentively around the long oak dining table as he replenished empty glasses.

The landlord had no need to worry unduly. Bliss was preoccupied, not only by the mellowing effect of the fine food and wine, but with the main business of the evening. Recent auction sales on the quayside of Wells, at which various lots of smuggled goods were sold to the highest bidders, had raised considerable cash sums for the Treasury. A generous percentage of the revenue thus engendered was set aside as prize-money for the main participants in the armed raids and seizures. There remained the exceedingly pleasant task of dividing the spoils, the lion's share of which would go to Bliss and the Army officers seated at the dining table. Suitable cash rewards, Bliss hoped, would filter through to the pockets of the sergeants, corporals and private dragoons who had provided sterling support on the village raids, and whose assistance had been of incalculable value. While Bliss had no authority to insist that such payments be made to the rank and file, or to intervene in internal Army matters, he made clear to the Officers present that the recent successful strike rate against the smuggling gangs was due largely to the high level of morale amongst the soldiers involved in the front line. On many future occasions, the same soldiers would be required to face the potentially murderous hordes in the coastal villages. Only by a fair apportionment of prize-money, Bliss argued, would the desired levels of discipline and morale be maintained.

Negotiations were interrupted by the approach to the dining table of a serving girl who, after apologies for the intrusion, delivered a written message addressed to Mr Bliss. The handwriting, barely literate, was instantly recognisable. Bliss made his excuses to the Dragoon Officers, rose from his chair and found his way to the rear door of the tavern. He walked to the stable yard and made uneasy forward progress as he met the full impact of a severe and bitterly cold north-easterly gale. Across the yard, he could just discern the silhouette of a strongly-built, well-clad figure, waiting by the door of the stables. On closer inspection, the only visible feature of the heavily disguised individual was a pair of hooded eyes, the gaze of which shifted nervously as the Excise man approached. Despite the lack of physical detail on display, Bliss knew at once that his uninvited visitor was the same informer who had provided valuable and accurate information on many previous meetings.

No time was wasted with pleasantries or greetings. Whilst his eyes darted in all directions, as if seeking reassurance that there were no witnesses to the brief discussion, the informer hastily provided details regarding significant quantities of smuggled goods, currently stored in the houses and backyards of two Thornham village residents. Bliss committed to memory the names of William Overton and William Southgate, the occupiers of the two premises allegedly storing contraband. In addition, Bliss was advised that Franklyn, his henchmen Bunkey and Summers, together with many of the local smuggling elite, were preparing to absent themselves from the village in order to celebrate both the New Year and the wedding of one of Franklyn's cousins in the port of King's Lynn. If Bliss were to raid the village of Thornham on New Year's Eve, the informer predicted, he would be unopposed. A profitable return was guaranteed. The meeting ended abruptly as the informer, without taking his leave, disappeared into the dark and stormy night. There had been no mention during the brief discourse of financial reward; money never changed hands at the initial stage of a deal. If all went well for Bliss, and the information proved to be accurate, then payment would be made to the informer, subject to a successful outcome, at a later date and after the raid.

Bliss returned to the Inn and rejoined the Dragoon Officers in the dining room. He picked up his glass of cognac, lit a pipe of tobacco and dragged his chair close to the hearth, to enjoy the warming comfort of the blazing log fire. He explained that during his brief absence, he had received information concerning significant quantities of smuggled tea and spirits presently concealed in Thornham village. He would require the services of the usual complement of reliable dragoons to help seize the contraband, on the morning of 31st December. Bliss's authority and reputation in North Norfolk was at its zenith; the Dragoon Officers, anticipating another profitable return from the deployment of their men and horses, agreed to the Exciseman's request, without question, qualification, or hesitation.

The morning of the last day of the year 1782 dawned bright, clear and frosty. The persistent northerly gales had at long last expended their energy, to be replaced by an air of calm that was strangely at odds with the scenes of destruction in the harbour, where broken masts, twisted ropes and tangled moorings testified to the power of the previous night's storm. Bliss surveyed the mayhem as he led his horse over the cobbled quayside, on his way to the stable yard behind the Fleece Inn, where his Dragoons were preparing for action. One corporal and six private soldiers were tending their horses and priming their weaponry, prior to Bliss's military style inspection. Also present in the yard were three subordinate Excise Officers, Messrs Abbott, Spencer and Banham who would join their Supervisor on what appeared to be a routine village raid. Carbines and pistols belonging to the small cavalry force were checked rigorously, with particular attention being given to fire-arms, powder, chambers and flints. Sabres were tested for ease of withdrawal from their scabbards. Once satisfied that everything was in perfect working order, Bliss gave the order to mount. The horses frisked excitedly, their hooves clattering with impatience and eagerness on the straw-strewn stone surface of the yard. Some reared on their hind legs; others jerked their heads against the tension of the reins and snorted small clouds of vapourized air through their flared nostrils. When order was restored, Bliss gave the order to proceed. The column of eleven men and horses, dominated by the colourful blue and yellow uniforms of the 11th Light Dragoon Regiment, moved away in single file, through the arch leading from stable yard to the highway, and took the western exit from the port, *en route* to Thornham.

Once outside the town, uneasy progress was made over the uneven, rutted tracks which linked all towns and villages in the coastal area. The initial route took the small troop past the northern perimeter fence of Holkham Park, then through the hamlet of Burnham Overy, across the old bridge spanning the river Burn, to the adjoining parishes of Burnham Ulph and Burnham Westgate.[1] At the Pitt Arms[2], Bliss brought the column to a halt and invited his Excise Officers and Dragoons to join him for refreshment at the Inn. It was customary for Bliss to encourage members of his raiding parties by providing, at his own expense, substantial nourishment for all concerned. It was a gesture appreciated especially by the Dragoons, who were accustomed to the poorest quality provisions served to them by their reluctant landlords, upon whom they were compulsorily billeted, at hostelries such as the Fleece in Wells. The Pitt Arms at Burnham Westgate was another such establishment on the War Office list of taverns required by law to provide food, lodgings and stabling to military detachments, for minimal financial compensation. The licensee, William Ballard, like others in his position, was careful in the extreme to provide modest sustenance, within the miserly War Office allocation of four pence per day, per soldier and horse. On this occasion, however, Mr Ballard's guest was a conscientious Exciseman, whose legal powers were greatly feared by local inn-keepers; in addition, Mr Bliss was paying a proper price for the fare on offer. The result, from the under-nourished Dragoons' point of view, was a gastronomic experience far exceeding their normal expectation.

The column of men and horses rode away from the Pitt Arms in good heart, passing the church of Burnham Westgate, where bell-ringers in the base of the west tower had already begun an ambitious and extended peal to celebrate the coming New Year. The repetitive sounds receded as progress was made over a remote track leading to the heathland of Burnham Deepdale Downs and Brancaster Common. From the peak of the ridge of high ground, Bliss scanned the view to the north, over Brancaster Bay and the seemingly endless expanse of the

[1] Three ancient parishes, Burnham Ulph, Burnham Sutton and Burnham Westgate have combined to form the present day small market town of Burnham Market. The churches of Burnham Ulph and Burnham Westgate remain, but the church of Burnham Sutton has long been in ruins.
[2] See footnote on p.24. The Pitt Arms was renamed the Hoste in the early nineteenth century.

German Ocean[1]. The sea was becalmed in the still air, its waters reflecting the deep blue of a cloudless sky. He produced a telescope from his saddle bag and focused on the vain attempts of numerous small, innocent-looking fishing smacks and merchant vessels to make progress. Sails hung from their mast-heads in limp, lazy and lifeless fashion, occasionally attracting a reluctant on-shore breeze, as the vessels tacked tediously in search of new water. It was a peaceful scene. Indeed, such was the tranquillity of the scene he surveyed that there was no indication of the problems awaiting the Exciseman in the hours to come.

The small cavalry force continued its journey, descending into the village of Brancaster, and turned left on to the wider coastal track which led through the hamlet of Titchwell and eventually to the eastern outskirts of Thornham, the most notorious village in the whole of Bliss's territory. Some of the horses reared and snorted, perhaps in anticipation of danger, as the column passed a farmyard on the left, the first sign of habitation in the infamous community. Opposite the farm, a small group of raggedly-attired children played noisily as they smashed and cracked the surface of an ice-covered pond. As the cavalry rode past, their excited squeals turned to silent curiosity. Bliss led his party down a track to the right known as Greenway, which led to the Old Harbour, passing another farmhouse at the junction. A herd of cattle gazed through the bars of a wooden gate as the horses cantered in single file past the home-stall. In the distance down the lane, the first of a group of houses and cottages in the vicinity of the Old Harbour Channel came into view; it was the residence of William Overton[2], whose name and place of abode had been divulged to Bliss by his informer in Wells. Bliss dismounted and knocked on the front door of Overton's house. Simultaneously, he ordered his troop to search the outbuildings and barns in the adjoining walled enclosure to the left of the house. When William Overton appeared at his front door, Bliss was surprised to find a man approaching seventy years of age; he had expected to confront a much younger man. Overton, in 18th-century social terms, was minor gentry; he owned his house and held the copyhold of a number of strips of land dispersed throughout the parish in the medieval fashion. Enclosure had not yet

[1] Cartographers up to the end of the 18th century used the name 'The German Ocean', or 'Mare Germanicus', to describe what is now known as the North Sea.
[2] William Overton's house stood on the site of the present Herga Cottage in Green Lane.

124

been sanctioned by Parliament for the parish of Thornham and its agriculture was still based on the ancient Open Field system[1]. Overton's relatively high status in the social order did not necessarily disqualify him from being connected with the smuggling business, either as a receiver of goods or as a provider of a temporary hiding-place for commodities in transit. Furthermore, Overton's house was situated on the fringe of Thornham's smuggling community, an area encompassing Oldfield Green and the Old Harbour Channel, which housed known, convicted smugglers such as the Jickling and Forshaw families. Robert Bliss, however, had his doubts about Overton's apparent complicity; those doubts were compounded when he observed an expression of horror and genuine surprise on the face of the old man when the Dragoons, after a very brief search in the outbuildings, strode across the yard carrying a total of eighteen bulky, oil-skin bags, each containing about twenty-six pounds weight of smuggled tea. In the course of his duties, Bliss had frequently encountered protestations of innocence, usually feigned, but sometimes genuine. On this occasion, Bliss was convinced that Overton was a victim of circumstance, and that the smuggled goods had been secreted, or even deliberately planted, without the old man's knowledge.

The modest seizure of tea was loaded by the Dragoons on to the backs of their horses tethered in Overton's enclosure. After assuring the old man that he would not face prosecution for concealing smuggled goods on his premises, Bliss led his troops back up the lane and turned right into Eastgate, *en route* to his next target, the premises of William Southgate at the western end of the village. Having considered turning back to Wells, in view of the possibly suspicious nature of the information that had led him to Overton's premises, Bliss decided instead to complete his business in the village; it was a fateful decision, and one he would regret. As he rode his horse carefully over the frozen rutted track which served as the main village highway, he observed the first sign of potential opposition to his current manoeuvres. So far, his party had encountered only an old man and a group of small children. As his troop approached the Red Cow alehouse[2], on the left side of the

[1] The Enclosure Act for Thornham was passed in 1797.
[2] The Red Cow was one of three taverns in existence in Thornham village, along with The Chequers and The King's Head. The Red Cow was renamed The Oak in 1862, de-licensed in 1892, and soon after used as a show-room for the Thornham Ironworkers. The building, much modified, stands to this day, and is known as Oak House.

street, the situation changed dramatically. In the forecourt, a dozen or so horses were tethered, and fed contentedly from nose-bags. From within the hostelry came the raucous sounds of carousing customers, but as the soldiers rode past, the merriment ceased. At the windows, a host of faces peered through the misted window panes. It was evident that Bliss and his cavalry were not unexpected. A minute later, the column of cavalry passed the Chequers ale-house, on the right of the street; the black and white sign-board hung haphazardly on one hinge, a victim of the recent ferocious winds. The reception from within the Chequers replicated that from within the Red Cow moments earlier; hostile faces watched the cavalry's progress, while outside, dismounted riders leaned across their horses' saddles, and watched silently. The hostile reception continued as Bliss led his men into Churchgate. Outside the King's Head alehouse, a sinister group of agricultural labourers had gathered, holding tankards of ale in one hand, whilst brandishing wooden clubs, whips and pitch-forks in the other. Of even more sinister appearance was the small group of well-dressed individuals on horse-back, wearing vizards and masks, and displaying pairs of pistols in their wide leather waist belts. Bliss realised that he had ridden into a carefully planned trap. Behind his column of men, the village army from the Red Cow, the Chequers and the King's Head joined forces to seal off any escape from Churchgate. For Bliss, turning back was not an option; resolutely, he led his hugely outnumbered cavalry towards the church pond, and turned left along the narrow lane leading to Southgate's premises. The massed ranks of drunken labourers on foot, led by the masked riders, followed in close pursuit. As Bliss passed the junction with Otter Lane, he observed that a primitively armed rabble had positioned itself in the narrow highway, blocking the escape route back to the main village street, while directly ahead, in front of Southgate's property[1], another band of armed men were waiting to confront the beleaguered Exciseman.

---

[1] William Southgate's premises consisted of a cottage, which exists today in the form of the original portion of The Lifeboat Inn, together with a smaller cottage at the rear, and two outhouses. Contrary to popular myth, the premises were not licensed until 1832, when one ground floor room was set aside for the consumption of home-brewed beer, on payment of two guineas per annum for an Excise Licence, under the terms of the 1830 Licensing Act. The Beer-house was then known as Pointers, after the first licensee Francis Pointer, who was primarily a local carrier. It was not until 1869, when John Sadler became licensee, that the Beer-house was first named The Lifeboat, probably in commemoration of the first Hunstanton Lifeboat launched two years previously.

The impending confrontation, between Bliss's small, inadequate force of eleven men, and the village horde numbering in excess of one hundred, was a direct result of the carefully formulated trap, prepared by Franklyn, which had lured Bliss into a hopeless and life-threatening situation. Neither Franklyn, nor his lieutenants, nor any of his supporters had absented themselves from the village, contrary to information given to Bliss at the Green Dragon in Wells a few days previously. Now Bliss was at the mercy of his adversary; in the harsh realities of eighteenth century life in general, and of smuggling confrontations in particular, the concept of mercy was a notably absent virtue. Bliss was about to experience vengeance from an enraged smuggling community; it would amount to a lesson he would never forget, and one from which he would never recover.

Bliss's cavalry had been split into two groups by the heaving mass of weapon-brandishing villagers. Directly in front of Southgate's cottage, Bliss, together with his three Excise Officers and two Dragoons, had been pushed back and surrounded by a mob of seventy to eighty hostile smugglers, all baying for blood like a pack of hounds. The six cornered men remained mounted, preferring the relative security afforded by their lofty position astride their horses. They grouped themselves into as tight and secure a unit as circumstances allowed; to a man they froze, almost motionless, fearful in the extreme lest the slightest movement should induce a surge of violent aggression from their tormentors. At some distance from the cottage, a smaller group of the pitchfork army had surrounded the five other Dragoons; leaderless and bewildered, the young soldiers held themselves firmly in their saddles, as the enemy prodded and spiked them with sadistic relish.

Franklyn had waited a long time for an opportunity to demonstrate his power to his opponents and supporters alike. With the odds stacked firmly in his favour, he rode confidently towards his adversary. The belligerent mob parted to allow him an avenue of access to Bliss and his Officers, who had been pushed back by force of numbers to the front door of Southgate's cottage. 'What? You six have come to rob us?', he asked mockingly, as he gestured with an expansive sweep of his arms in the direction of his massive following. 'We shall murder you all!'[1] It was

---

[1] Dragoon Sergeant Boutell testified in his Court Deposition that these were the precise words used by Franklyn.

no idle threat; in an instant, Franklyn grabbed the reins of the Exciseman's horse, and pulled his victim within striking range. With his other hand, he snatched a heavy bludgeon from one of his henchmen and, with horrendous force, struck a violent blow to the side of Bliss's face. Bliss slumped forward over his horse's neck; as he struggled, severely dazed, to regain an upright position in the saddle, the offensive end of a lead-loaded whip wrapped its disfiguring tentacle around his head. It bit deeply into his eye-socket. Franklyn, with obsessive savagery, bludgeoned his enemy's skull with further repeated blows. Once again, Bliss fell forward, his facial features hidden by a mass of blood which oozed freely from wounds to the top of his head and from both sides of his face.

The beatings would have continued until death, had not Sergeant Boutell of the 11th Dragoons intervened. The sergeant, a veteran amongst novices, assumed control of the fearful events unfolding before him; further delay would have invited a certain massacre. He drew his sabre, a thirty-seven-inch blade sharpened to effect the most appalling physical injury, took a firm hold of the reins of Bliss's horse, dug his heels into the flanks of his own mount, and rode a direct course of escape through the ranks of the enemy, dragging his unconscious leader behind him. Encouraged by the Sergeant's positive action, the rest of the Dragoon and Excise cavalry followed in swift pursuit. The village army fell back, fearful of the consequences of obstructing a tormented quarry which, at last, was in a position to retaliate and to release its frustration and extreme anger. Heads, limbs and chests of many village men were hideously lacerated as the fleeing column slashed their sabres with vengeful ferocity at anyone within reach. The lane immediately in front of Southgate's cottage was left littered with writhing bodies, screaming and bloodied, some scarred and incapacitated for life. Silver icy patches of the frozen, rutted highway contrasted vividly with crimson rivulets of blood seeping from severe and untended injuries. Many of the suffering had come merely to make up the numbers and to enjoy an afternoon of festive fun at the expense of the hated Excise; full of alcohol, they had been too slow to remove themselves from the worst excesses of Sergeant Boutell and his professionally-trained cavalry as they made their escape from a desperate situation.

Franklyn and five of his closest henchmen gave chase to the departing cavalry, through the lanes and streets of Thornham, and through the villages of Titchwell, Brancaster and Burnham Deepdale, as far as the outskirts of Burnham Westgate. Although fire-arms were occasionally discharged, causing no damage other than shot-holes in Excise Officer Abbott's coat-tails, the pursuit was more a gesture of defiance than an expression of intent. Of the original seizure from William Overton's premises[1] of eighteen bags of tea, all but six had been recovered by the smugglers during the affray and subsequent pursuit. The loss of the greater part of the seizure was of little consequence to the Excisemen; foremost in their minds was the deteriorating physical condition of Robert Bliss. Their leader had suffered severe loss of blood during and after the succession of frenzied assaults. Slumped over his horse's neck, held in the saddle by one of his subordinates, Bliss held on to life by a thread. The ride to Burnham Westgate, home of the nearest surgeon, was not ideal; the constant buffeting whilst astride a horse did nothing to stem the flow of blood. Strips of cloth had been tied around his skull as a temporary expedient, but urgent medical attention was imperative if his life were to be saved. Meanwhile, the chasing pack of smugglers, led by Franklyn, continued to harass the rear of the retreating column of cavalry, occasionally beating the hind-most dragoon and periodically picking up bags of discarded contraband. Where the highway widened at the approach to Burnham Westgate, Sergeant Boutell was able to organise his men into an attacking formation. A line of six Dragoons turned and faced the enemy; on Boutell's command, they raised their carbines and simultaneously fired a volley at their pursuers. The warning shots, aimed deliberately high, had the desired effect. Franklyn and his henchmen, allergic as ever to adverse odds, turned tail and retreated to Thornham, in a mood of satisfaction with the course of the day's events. By contrast, the Excise party limped dejectedly into Burnham Westgate. The column halted in front of Surgeon Thomas Rand's house; Robert Bliss was lifted carefully from his blood-soaked saddle and was carried by four dragoons into the sanctuary of the

1 It is not known whether William Southgate was concealing smuggled commodities, knowingly or otherwise, as Bliss's raiding party was attacked before a search of his premises and outbuildings could be instigated. Southgate was a fisherman who was in financial difficulties, to such an extent that he had mortgaged his property, consisting of the original portion of the present day Lifeboat Inn, a cottage at the rear, and two barns, for £100 in 1781. It is not unreasonable to suppose that Southgate would willingly have concealed smuggled goods in his premises, in return for appropriate cash inducement.

Surgery. The Surgeon's immediate diagnosis was unfavourable. With luck, Bliss would survive, but his ability to lead future armed incursions against smugglers would be seriously compromised. The beatings he had suffered would leave him permanently blinded in one eye; sight in the other would be, at best, impaired.

With such sombre news, the Excise party returned slowly and wearily to Wells. The final day of the year had dawned favourably for the Exciseman; as dusk fell, he lay unconscious, in the care of a Surgeon, his life in the balance, his future, if he survived, uncertain.

A VILLAGE IN TERROR

There were no celebrations in Thornham on New Year's Day, 1783. Rumour was rife, throughout the village, of imminent mass arrests, by government forces, of the participants in the previous day's violence. Those seriously injured by the escaping cavalry experienced agonies both physical and mental; if the searing pain of lacerated limbs were not bad enough, then the fear of arrest for obvious complicity, on account of their sabre-wounds, compounded their anxiety. Neither had the wealthier residents of the village slept easily in their beds. Civil unrest on the scale demonstrated by the labouring classes of Thornham had given the local gentry cause for great concern and mounting fear. While they were happy to stock the cellars of their fine houses with exquisite wines and spirits, and for their ladies to wear quality silks, purchased at a fraction of their market price, the landowners and merchants of the village realised that mass violence, on the scale directed against the Excise, was only a small step away from social and political insurrection. Such a development, clearly, was not in their best interests.

Henry Benton and Thomas Willis were two such residents, who occupied newly constructed mansions[1] and were vessel-owning merchants and land-owning farmers. Both men had accumulated considerable wealth. On the morning of January 2nd, they rode to the Excise Office in Wells to express their fears that the recent Excise raid

[1] Henry Benton owned the Red House, and Thomas Willis the Hall. Both splendid houses were designed for their merchant owners and exist to this day. They feature sea-facing observation garrets specifically designed to overlook the Thornham Old and New Harbours.

had caused great resentment in their village, and that the mood of the labouring classes was, to say the least, volatile. Consequently, they were greatly concerned for the safety of their persons, their families and, not least, their properties. The complaints expressed by the two Thornham merchants were not well received at the Excise Office, where prevailed a vehement sense of outrage at the events which had so critically incapacitated Robert Bliss, and where a determination by the Officers for revenge against the perpetrators was clearly in evidence. William Spencer had just returned from Burnham Westgate, where he had attended a bed-side meeting at the Surgeon's house with his Supervisor. Spencer delivered the news that, as a result of the meeting, letters had already been despatched by riders to the Sheriff of Norfolk, requesting a signed warrant for the arrest of Thomas Franklyn, and to Excise headquarters in London, demanding that a resident peace-keeping military force be sent to Thornham, to quell the revolutionary fervour of the lower orders. The letter to Excise headquarters, drafted and written by Spencer, but signed in a barely legible scrawl by the ailing Bliss, read:-

The Excise Office, Wells juxta Mare,
Norfolk.
2nd January 1783

Honourable Sirs,

I received information of smuggled goods being lodged at Thornham in this district, to which place I proceeded with a party of Dragoons, and seized eighteen quarter bags of tea. The Dragoons giving way to a gang of smugglers, part of the goods were rescued, myself cruelly beat, having five wounds in my head, and no sight of one eye, and but very little from the other, humbly pray your Honours leave to be absent from business eight or ten days to recover myself from the loss of blood which was very great.
I have proceeded in accordance with the Smuggling Act of 1746 against those offenders, the particulars of which will be forwarded as soon as sight will permit.
I humbly pray that an Order may be obtained for a military force to be sent to Thornham, there being three public houses known as the 'Kings Head', the 'Chequer' and the 'Red Cow' that often entertain between twenty and thirty smugglers and their horses, at each house.

I am
Your Honours servant
Robert Bliss

The Smuggling Act of 1746, which Bliss and his Excise colleagues were preparing to invoke in order to deal with the miscreants of Thornham, contained highly oppressive and fiercely punitive terms of reference. Incorporating clauses from previous legislation, as well as introducing new provisions, the 1746 Act was far-reaching, and its terms were particularly relevant to the recent riotous events in Thornham on New Year's Eve. It stipulated that the wounding of a Customs or Excise Officer in the execution of his duty was punishable on conviction by death. Persons assembling for the purpose of running contraband were no longer to be transported, but to be hanged instead. There were also provisions for collective financial penalties upon whole communities in the event of riotous assembly. Alehouse keepers who entertained smugglers on their premises were to be fined £100, and were to forfeit their licences. Equally alarming from the smuggling community's viewpoint were the sections of the Act which actively encouraged smugglers to turn 'King's evidence', and to divulge to the authorities the names of their fellow activists. Anyone who came forward with information leading to the arrest and conviction of a colleague would obtain a free pardon for his past crimes, together with a handsome cash reward.

If the purpose of this inducement to inform was to undermine the spirit and togetherness of closely-knit smuggling communities, it succeeded in the village of Thornham. Speculation, rumour and hysteria engulfed the entire population. Confusion and suspicion disrupted normal village life; whispers of betrayals and informers abounded. Inevitably, neighbours, friends, even families became divided by mutual distrust. Within days, the situation deteriorated further. In early January, The War Office ordered a detachment of twenty men and horses belonging to the 20th Regiment of Light Dragoons, quartered in King's Lynn, to take up billets in the immediate Thornham area. Six dragoons were detached to Old Hunstanton, and a further six to Docking; four were sent to Holme and four more to Heacham. On the same day, another troop of the same Regiment, quartered in Bury St Edmunds, was ordered to despatch an officer and sixteen men to Thornham, where they were 'to remain until further notice, to assist Officers of the Revenue to apprehend smugglers'. The War Office had reacted speedily to Bliss's letter to Excise headquarters, containing his version of events on New Year's Eve, and to his plea for help. The Government was clearly alarmed; although civil disturbance was commonplace in cities and towns throughout the country, it was unusual for a major insurrection to occur in an under-populated, rural and isolated region such as north-west Norfolk. Even so, similarly non-strategic regions had experienced comparable clashes between smuggling gangs and Revenue forces, without prompting an authoritarian back-lash from central government in the form of the imposition of a major military presence. Perhaps Westminster feared that the recent violent disturbances were prompted by agitators with social and political motives, rather than by local smugglers wishing to settle an old score with Revenue Officers.

Whatever the reasons behind the decision to surround and infiltrate the village with Government troops, the residents of Thornham felt an immediate impact. As a column of sixteen mounted dragoons, led by an Officer, rode into the village in impressive style and with an arrogant demeanour, other sinister elements arrived in its wake. The Sheriff of Norfolk sent two of his bailiffs armed with warrants for arrest, while a contingent of the feared and despised Naval Press Gang arrived, brandishing weaponry of a more rudimentary and intimidating nature. The bailiffs had been instructed to arrest anyone involved in the New Year's Eve attack on Bliss and his raiding cavalry, provided that sworn statements proving their involvement could be obtained, by whatever means, from other villagers or witnesses. Orders given to the Press-gang were less complicated and involved no paper work; any able-bodied male between the ages of eighteen and forty, whose direct complicity in the affray was difficult to prove, was to be forcibly apprehended, taken to King's Lynn, and pressed into active service on one of His Majesty's Naval vessels. Customary recruiting grounds for the Press Gang, such as the harbour and the alehouses, were deserted. So too were the village streets, as males both young and old confined themselves to the relative security of their houses. Even behind bolted doors and windows, they felt insecure; some travelled to neighbouring villages, to hide and await information that it was safe to return. Others secreted themselves in out-houses, barns, cattle-sheds, underground vaults, or any of the traditional hiding places much used by a community which thrived on smuggling.

For all the villagers, whether or not they were complicit in the barbaric assaults on Bliss and his cavalry, it was a desperately harrowing time. By contrast, the dragoon soldiers drafted into the village were able to enjoy an unusual freedom from local hostility, as nobody in the village dared challenge their authority for fear of arrest; furthermore, they were able to commandeer the three alehouses for their own personal and domestic use. Even the licensees, upon whom they were compulsorily billeted, were hospitable, outwardly at least. Fearful of official retribution for past misdemeanours, such as harbouring smugglers on their premises, fearful too of crippling fines and of forfeiting their licences, the alehouse-keepers at the King's Head, the Chequers and the Red Cow entertained the rank-and-file dragoons with quality food and plentiful porter ale, regardless of cost and profit margins. In the absence of a village inn to provide suitably salubrious lodgings befitting a gentleman, the Officer commanding the dragoons was accommodated at the Red House by Henry Benton who, as ever, was anxious to find favour with authority in troubled times.

Meanwhile, the agents of governmental authority – the Navy Press Gang, the Sheriff's bailiffs and constables, the Army's dragoons – went about their separate business unopposed. Immediately, all smuggling activity in the village and in the surrounding area was curtailed, at least temporarily. More seriously, an unknown number of male residents were taken by force from their native village by the Press Gang to a life of brutality aboard Navy warships. A further ten local men, all fringe members of Franklyn's village army, were apprehended by dragoon soldiers and arrested by the Sheriff's bailiffs on charges of obstructing Excise Officers, of being 'armed with offensive weapons, to wit guns, blunderbusses, pistols, bludgeons, pitch-forks and pea-hooks', and of unlawful, riotous and felonious assembly. All were taken to Norwich and imprisoned in the County Gaol at the Castle, to await trial at the forthcoming Lent Assizes at Thetford in March.

Whilst abductions and arrests became common in his adopted village, and while terror of his own making reigned unhindered, Franklyn remained a free man. Anticipating the troubled course of events, he had removed himself from the immediate area and had gone to ground in the back-street warrens and yards of the North End fishing community, in the parish of St Nicholas, in his native King's Lynn.

THE ARREST OF THOMAS FRANKLYN

Reports of the alarming recent events in Thornham village made little impression on Thomas Franklyn; indeed, his behaviour after returning to familiar surroundings in King's Lynn suggests that he believed himself to be immune from serious legal retribution. It was an attitude adopted by many of his contemporaries who had achieved both financial success and social infamy through the smuggling business. As we have seen, Franklyn was accustomed to assaulting Officers of the Preventive Service; in his mind, Robert Bliss was simply another name to add to his growing list of battered victims. Franklyn clearly assumed that, even if he were to be charged with the recently committed offences, he would face no more than a Quarter Sessions hearing before a sympathetic local Justice of the Peace, in his home town, and would probably receive, by way of punishment, no more than the usual derisory fine. It would appear that he hadn't even considered the possibility of being taken to the County Assizes to face trial by Circuit Judge and Jury for offences which, on conviction, were punishable by death.

In King's Lynn on the morning of 6th January 1783, while mass arrests were taking place in remote Thornham, the seemingly carefree Franklyn attended the marriage ceremony in St Nicholas Chapel of Robert Watson, a distant kinsman. He spent the remainder of the daylight hours drinking in numerous alehouses in nearby Dowshill Street[1] and Hogman's Lane[2], in celebration of the wedding and in the company of his two henchmen, Bunkey and Summers. As darkness fell, a small group of individuals of menacing countenance gathered furtively in a gloomy side alley off Hogman's Lane, within view of Franklyn's house. One was dressed in the habit of a civilian Peace-officer, while three other men wore the blue jackets, white trousers and pigtails which signified a naval connection. The Peace-officer was one Thomas Allen of the parish of Gaywood; he had been selected recently by the Sheriff of Norfolk as a special bailiff and had been charged with the responsibility of serving an arrest warrant upon Thomas Franklyn and of taking him into custody.

---

[1] Dowshill Street was renamed at a later date, and is now known as Pilot Street. See map of King's Lynn overleaf showing the layout of streets in the eighteenth century.
[2] Hogman's Lane was renamed at a later date, and is now known as Austin Street.

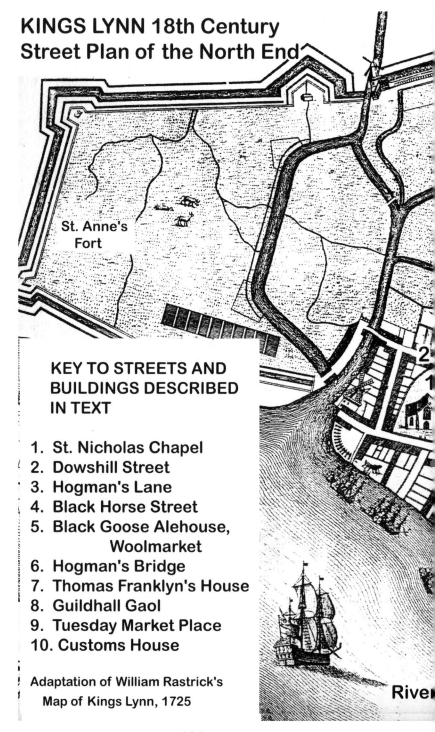

KINGS LYNN 18th Century
Street Plan of the North End

St. Anne's
Fort

KEY TO STREETS AND
BUILDINGS DESCRIBED
IN TEXT

1. St. Nicholas Chapel
2. Dowshill Street
3. Hogman's Lane
4. Black Horse Street
5. Black Goose Alehouse,
      Woolmarket
6. Hogman's Bridge
7. Thomas Franklyn's House
8. Guildhall Gaol
9. Tuesday Market Place
10. Customs House

Adaptation of William Rastrick's
  Map of Kings Lynn, 1725

River

Market
Cross

9

8

10

The
Purfleet

Ouse

137

To assist him in performing this daunting task, Thomas Allen recruited the services of John Mundford, John Cook and Thomas Hays, all of whom were members of the Port of King's Lynn Press Gang. All four men were suitably armed for the task and carried the heavy-headed bludgeons much favoured by members of the Navy's ruthless recruitment squad[1]. The sinister group lingered patiently in the shadows of the dingy neighbourhood until, at about six o'clock in the evening, Franklyn was observed leaving an alehouse in Hogman's Lane. The solitary figure made erratic and stumbling progress across the rubbish-strewn surface of the cobbled street. In an instant, and to his great surprise, he was surrounded by the four men. Thomas Allen grabbed and held his collar with a strong-fisted grip, while the Press Gang secured him by the arms. A combination of natural belligerence, wounded pride and an advanced state of inebriation combined to produce from Franklyn a predictable response. Using his unfettered legs to kick wildly, stallion-like, in all directions, and employing every muscle of his powerful frame, he broke free from his captors. As he did so, he bellowed and roared with as much vocal force as his lungs could muster, to relieve his raging temper as much as to summon his friends in the immediate vicinity. His entourage, alerted by the excessive noise, duly arrived, and within seconds a mob numbering more than twenty arrived on the scene, led by Bunkey and Summers brandishing bludgeons above their heads. Hugely outnumbered, Peace-officer Allen and his assistants retreated slowly by stepping backwards, thereby keeping the mob in view, at the same time showing little enthusiasm for a one-sided conflict.

Franklyn, Bunkey and Summers, followed by their supporters, wandered defiantly away from their reluctant adversaries and returned to the alehouse in Dowshill Street. Thomas Allen and his Pressmen persevered with their task, and waited for an opportunity to strike again. This time their victim was Summers who interrupted his celebrations by staggering from within the ill-lit hostelry in order to urinate in the

---

[1] Pistols and carbines were not part of the Press Gang's customary weaponry. Discharging only a single lead ball between time-consuming re-loads, firearms were also unreliable and inaccurate. More importantly, to kill or permanently incapacitate a conscript was counter-productive; it made more sense to concuss a potential recruit temporarily with an expertly executed blow to the skull, so that the victim would be ready for active service within a relatively short space of time.

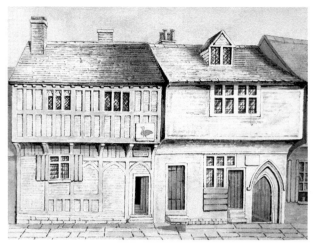

The Black Goose alehouse, Woolmarket, King's Lynn with painted signboard above the entrance. The Gothic archway on the adjoining building to the right remains to this day. The Black Goose was the favoured haunt of the Press Gang in the 1780s.

The Press Gang or Impress Service from a caricature of 1780. The gangs, each led by a Regulating Officer, operated in all English ports in the 18th century to enlist unwilling recruits to the Royal Navy. Gangers, armed with clubs, were paid up to 10s per victim. They also accepted bribes from wealthy targeted victims, who would pay handsomely to remain at liberty from impressment.

street. At such a vulnerable moment, he was easily overpowered and was force-marched in the direction of the town gaol at the Guildhall. Once again, the attempted arrest was foiled. In Black Horse Street[1], the pursuing Franklyn and his fellow revellers overtook Allen and his accomplices, and challenged them to release their prisoner. Without waiting for a response, Franklyn launched himself into a ferocious assault on John Mundford. A violent blow to the head from a heavy bludgeon caused the Officer of the Press Gang to relinquish his grip on Summers, and to fall backwards against a wall in a semi-conscious daze. Immediately, Franklyn disabled John Cook with a similarly vicious strike. As Summers regained his liberty, a jubilant Franklyn taunted his opponents for their lack of courage and their numerical inferiority. 'Now damn you, ye buggers', he exclaimed, 'go fetch some more of ye'[2].

Thomas Allen and his battered assistants retired to the Black Goose alehouse in Woolmarket[3], to recover from their beatings and to decide how best to ensnare their hot-tempered quarry. Allen hoped to recruit further members of the Press Gang to his cause, as it was now apparent that the only way of successfully serving the arrest warrant was to increase the manpower at his disposal. Franklyn, it seemed, was able to call on the protection of the entire party of drunken wedding guests, together with an unknown number of disaffected mariners and petty criminals who infested the streets in the port's immediate vicinity. At the Black Goose, a regular meeting place and unofficial local headquarters of the port's Press Gang, Allen found one Thomas Braddock, a Press-officer of particularly belligerent demeanour and reputation. Braddock was instantly enlisted. However, with two of his contingent less than fully operational, as a result of Franklyn's assaults, Allen had no alternative but to call in the assistance of the West Norfolk Militia.

[1] Black Horse Street was the popular, alternative name for Listergate Street, and was so named after the Black Horse alehouse on its eastern side. The street was later renamed Chapel Street, as it is known today.
[2] These were the precise words used by Franklyn, according to the written and signed depositions of Allen, Mundford, Cook and Hays, taken on oath, 3rd February 1783.
[3] Woolmarket was later renamed St Nicholas Street, by which name it is known today. The Black Goose was sited on the south side of the street, in the area now used as a car park. The original street side doorway remains to this day, in the form of a solitary Gothic arch.

Such an option had been available to him from the outset, but it was with good reason that Allen initially dismissed it as potentially counter-productive. The Militia was a part time force of conscripted, mainly youthful and usually reluctant amateurs, of little experience and of dubious quality. The conscripts were chosen at random by ballot from the County's parishes, to compensate for the absence of regular Army forces called abroad in times of war. Their officers were no more effective: selected from families of local squires and landowners, they were at best enthusiastic, but in practice were even more incompetent than their counterparts in the regular Army. In order to complete his task, Allen would have preferred to have the backing of a dozen or so purposeful and professional Pressmen, but it was not to be. With great reluctance, therefore, he despatched Hays to the guard house at St Anne's Fort, close by St Nicholas' Chapel, where a party of the Militia was garrisoned. Hays was instructed to direct the Militiamen to a rendezvous in Hogman's Lane, near Hogman's Bridge, where Allen, Mundford, Cook and Braddock would await their arrival.

At about 10 o'clock in the evening, fourteen foot soldiers of the Militia marched through the gates of St Anne's Fort. Commanding Officer Lieutenant Colonel Gabbett seized the opportunity to demonstrate his importance to the townspeople of King's Lynn by personally leading his men on the short journey to Hogman's Bridge. He rode on horseback, at the head of the column. Behind him, a sergeant dictated the marching pace with vocal commands, as he strove in vain to keep his charges in step, in true military fashion. The procession was chaotic, even comical. Wearing ill-fitting footwear and uniforms, carrying weapons to which they were unaccustomed, the boy-soldiers stumbled over the uneven surface of the narrow cobbled streets as they tried to keep pace with the marching orders of their sergeant. The ragged column passed numerous alehouses *en route*, to the great amusement of drunken mariners within. Verbal abuse, ribaldry and mockery were unabated, as the ill-disciplined and poorly trained conscripts arrived at their destination with an appearance which was far short of intimidating. On seeing the rabble arrive at Hogman's Bridge, Thomas Allen's worst fears were realised. To make matters even worse, the Lieutenant Colonel, who was undeterred by, and seemingly oblivious to, the shambles in his wake, immediately announced his intention of taking command of the entire operation.

King's Lynn from the west, showing the North End of the town and port in the early 18th century. The spire of St Nicholas Chapel dominates merchants' houses and warehouses flanking the waterfront. Purfleet Quay and the Customs House are at the extreme right of the view.

Behind the river front, a warren of narrow streets, alehouses and terraced dwellings harboured a community of smugglers, pressmen, mariners and violent criminals. *Drawing by Henry Bell.*

The combined forces of Thomas Allen and the Lieutenant Colonel proceeded to a narrow *cul-de-sac* off Hogman's Lane and arrived outside Franklyn's house, where all the wedding guests had assembled to continue the post-nuptials. Astonishingly, Franklyn continued to dismiss the serious threat to his liberty, despite the considerable manpower and weaponry assembled on his door-step. It was a foolish error of judgement; the Militia may have consisted of raw and untrained recruits, but every soldier was armed with a potentially lethal carbine and other assorted firearms. In addition, Lieutenant Colonel Gabbett was eager to show off his supposed military prowess and nothing less than a violent and ultimately successful engagement would satisfy his vanity. Despite the Officer's impatience to involve all his Militia from the outset, it was Thomas Allen who took the initiative. With Braddock at his side, he entered Franklyn's house through the front door, which invitingly was unlocked, and at the same time ordered four soldiers to take up position at the back of the house, to guard the rear exit. The Lieutenant Colonel was left high and dry in the saddle, temporarily upstaged; his moment of glory would surely come.

Allen and Braddock crept stealthily along a narrow hallway, at the end of which a semi-opaque glass door offered the spectacle of a tightly-packed gathering of merry-makers, some drinking, others dancing to the lively sounds of a fiddle. Similar sounds of merriment emanated from the upstairs rooms. The entire interior was ill-lit, relying on occasional whale-oil lamps to cast flickering images of highlight and shadow. As the glass door in front of the two men slowly opened, sufficient light fell upon the features of Thomas Franklyn for Allen to recognise instantly his quarry. The process of recognition was mutual. Franklyn's instant reaction was to pick up and raise to his shoulder a loaded blunderbuss and to point the barrel unerringly in Allen's direction. Both Allen and Braddock dived to the floor in an instinctive act of self-preservation, as the blunderbuss discharged its barrel of ammunition above their heads. Outside the house, the Lieutenant Colonel heard the explosion of gun-fire, and reacted instantly. Without regard for the safety of the innocent revellers or indeed for his colleagues within the house, he bellowed the order to commence firing to eight of his soldiers positioned in readiness. A ferocious, reckless and indiscriminate volley of lead balls smashed through the front windows of the house. Some embedded themselves in the ceilings and interior walls; others, inevitably, tore holes in human

Left: Thomas de Gray, of Merton Hall, MP for Norfolk from 1764 to 1774, in heroic pose. He wears the uniform of a Lieut. Colonel of the West Norfolk Militia in the 1770s. His successor, Lieut. Col. Gabbett, commanded the violent siege of Thomas Franklyn's house in King's Lynn, which led to the smuggler's arrest.

Right: A private soldier of the West Norfolk Militia, c. 1800, carrying a 'Brown Bess' single-shot, smoothbore musket, much favoured by British infantry regiments throughout the 18th century. He wears the distinctive 'stove-pipe' shako on his head. A volley of 'Brown Bess' musket fire from eight such militiamen effectively ended the siege of Franklyn's house in King's Lynn's North End.

flesh. A woman was seriously injured by a lead bullet which passed through her upper arm; the festering wound led subsequently to the limb being amputated. Another woman survived miraculously as a bullet grazed her temple above the right eye. A tailor by the name of Nicholls was not so fortunate; he was shot through the heart, and died instantly.

The Lieutenant Colonel's heavy-handed action proved decisive. All resistance was broken by his brutal but effective tactics. Thomas Franklyn attempted a last-ditch attempt to escape via the roof-top, but was overpowered by Braddock in the act of clambering through a rear upstairs window. After a brief struggle, in which all four members of the Press Gang joined with predictable violence, Franklyn was secured with ankle and wrist chains and was hauled, bruised and senseless, down the stairs and into the street. The Militia and Press Gang, led by a triumphant Lieutenant Colonel Gabbett, escorted the prisoner as he was dragged over the cobbled streets to the town gaol at the Guildhall.

The evening's work was done.

THE DECLINE OF FRANKLYN AND BLISS

Two days later, news of Franklyn's arrest reached Thornham village, where it was received with considerable satisfaction throughout the small community. Franklyn had alienated even his most loyal supporters by fleeing the village before the arrival of the dragoon detachment, the Sheriff's bailiffs and the contingent of the Press Gang, and by leaving his previously devoted followers to face the consequences of the events of New Year's Eve. In addition, there was intense speculation that Franklyn or his henchmen had passed to the authorities the names of the ten Thornham men who had been arrested, and who still languished in the County Gaol at Norwich Castle, awaiting trial at the forthcoming County Assizes at Thetford in March. Franklyn himself spent two nights in the King's Lynn Guildhall Gaol, after which he was brought before Martin Ffolkes Rishton, a local Justice of the Peace. After hearing evidence given by Sergeant Boutell, Thomas Abbott and William Spencer, all three of whom had been present on the occasion of Franklyn's assault on Robert Bliss, Rishton duly and formally committed Franklyn to Norwich Castle, where he also would be confined until the Assizes commenced in two months' time.

Thornham village, along with its neighbours Old Hunstanton, Docking, Holme and Heacham, continued to experience a heavy military presence until the end of January 1783 when, to the immense relief of everyone except the wealthier residents, the dragoons were withdrawn. Their departure coincided with further good news. The ten Thornham labourers were released without charge from Norwich Castle gaol, on the grounds of there being insufficient evidence to convict them. Excise Officers Abbott and Spencer, and Sergeant Boutell had failed to identify positively any of those arrested, when they visited the County Gaol on behalf of the Prosecution. There were more compelling reasons for the villagers' early release. The authorities, having succeeded in arresting a prominent smuggling baron, would now be free to channel all their efforts into securing Franklyn's conviction and, hopefully, his execution.

Franklyn was taken from the Guildhall Gaol in King's Lynn to Norwich Castle by a heavily armed contingent of the West Norfolk Militia. As he would have only a few weeks to organise his defence before being brought to trial, he wasted no time in briefing a solicitor and in setting in motion the buying of witnesses, which was common practice in the shady world of smuggling. So many sympathisers came forward, mainly from King's Lynn, who were prepared to commit perjury on Franklyn's behalf for financial reward, that the trial, held on March 14th, lasted an astonishing seven hours. A seemingly endless procession of witnesses testified that Franklyn was not in Thornham on the afternoon of 31 December, as against only three men, Messrs Abbott, Spencer and Boutell, who provided contradictory testimony on behalf of the Prosecution. Crucially, Robert Bliss did not attend the trial. Although his physical wounds had begun to heal, apart from the permanent and complete loss of sight in one eye, his mental faculties appeared to have deserted him. His reasoning was apparently so confused that he was unable, eleven weeks after the assault, to contemplate even returning to his duties in Wells, let alone testifying in Court and coping with aggressive interrogation from the Defence Counsel.

In the event, the Prosecution case, which was at best ill-prepared, was overwhelmed completely by perjured evidence. The Prosecution also reckoned without having to deal with a biased jury of Norfolk men, all twelve of whom were seemingly sympathetic to the smuggling cause. The unanimous verdict of 'Not Guilty' was merely a precursor to that delivered in even more outrageous circumstances two years later, when Kemball and Gunton, as we have seen, were acquitted.

Franklyn's acquittal at the Thetford Assizes brought a muted response from the county's two major weekly newspapers. The *Norfolk Chronicle* reported the bare facts in a dispassionately brief manner, while the *Norwich Mercury* failed even to mention the verdict. Nevertheless, the trial signalled the end of Franklyn's career as a major player in the smuggling business. Additionally, the authorities, having failed to take his life, succeeded in squeezing him financially, by serving a succession of Exchequer writs, which extracted massive fines from his diminishing cash resources. His business empire in North Norfolk was completely dismantled, mainly because his local armies of village men no longer trusted him, and withdrew their support and their names from his pay-roll. He was reduced to a forlorn figure, who continued to indulge in small-time smuggling activity around the port and town of King's Lynn, and continued to engage in violent clashes with those in authority. Regular appearances at the King's Lynn Quarter Sessions throughout the years 1783 and 1784, for assaults against Excise Officers, Customs Officers, and on one occasion an Officer of the Royal Navy, testify to an unquenchable fighting spirit; but his heyday was over.

If Franklyn's star was in the descendant, so too was that of his great enemy, Robert Bliss. The Exciseman's absence from duty throughout January, February and March was treated sympathetically by his employers at Excise Headquarters, although disappointment was expressed at his failure to attend the Thetford Assizes. Sympathy gave way to irritation when his sick-leave extended to the end of July; an official entry in the Excise Board's Minutes of 29 July makes reference, with a degree of sarcasm, to Bliss being 'too ill' to return to active service. His symptoms indicated that Bliss was suffering acutely from severe mental and physical problems, following the savagely inflicted head wounds he received in Thornham at the hands of Franklyn; nevertheless, there was little sympathy for, or understanding of, such conditions at a time when medical knowledge was limited and its practices primitive. In August 1783, Bliss formally requested a transfer from Wells. His request was duly granted, on condition that he returned to duty immediately, as Supervisor of the Chelsea District in the Surrey Collection. Few details of his career on the fringe of the Metropolis were recorded. The posting was potentially dangerous, in view of the considerable volume of smuggling traffic which would have passed through the Chelsea District, on the journey from the West Sussex and Hampshire coasts to central London. However, there is no evidence to suggest that Bliss adopted the confrontational tactics which characterised his term of office in North Norfolk.

On the contrary, it would appear that Bliss had surrendered both physically and emotionally, and was no longer inclined to carry the fight to the enemy. His inactivity was clearly apparent to his employers at Excise Headquarters. In November 1785, his conduct was subjected to official scrutiny, when 'his prospects for preferment were curtailed', according to Excise Board minutes. The following year, official warnings were issued, and in 1787, his career with the Excise came to a sad and inappropriate end, when he was dismissed from service, without a pension, without compensation for injuries sustained in the course of duty, and without recognition for past achievements.

AFTERMATH

The massive scale of insurrection and riotous assembly at Thornham village on New Year's Eve 1782, together with numerous other confrontations between civilian armies and Government forces, particularly in the vicinity of the Kent and Sussex coasts, necessitated a positive response from a beleaguered government. As a direct result of such widespread civil unrest, a Commission of Enquiry into all aspects of the smuggling malaise was instigated by Lord Shelbourne during his brief term of office as Prime Minister in 1783. The Commission's report led to further and more repressive anti-smuggling legislation the following year. Prominent in the Commission's exhaustive catalogue of outrages perpetrated by smuggling gangs was the 'battle' of Thornham, which was reported to have involved 'in excess of three hundred labourers of lawless disposition sympathetic to the smuggling cause', and resulted in 'hideous injuries to an Officer of Excise'.

It was certainly the most serious demonstration of force perpetrated by civilians against government forces north of the Thames Estuary, and for this reason the remote corner of Norfolk coastline containing the villages of Thornham, Holme and Old Hunstanton was deliberately and routinely targeted throughout the remainder of the 1780s by officers of the Army and the Navy, and by officers of the Customs and the Excise. In effect, the three villages had gained an unenviable reputation for lawlessness and were selected for special, heavy-handed attention.

Throughout the remainder of the year 1783, seizures of hidden smuggled goods by Customs Officers and Excise Officers, supported by personnel from the 15th and 20th Light Dragoon Regiments, became almost a routine exercise. Every village along the coast from Heacham to Brancaster felt the effects of an authoritarian back-lash. The most significant confrontation occurred, once again, in the village of Thornham. In November, a huge consignment of brandy and Geneva was landed from a smuggling cutter on the beach between Holme and Thornham. William Turner, the Excise Superintendent from King's Lynn, recovered 125 of the landed half-anker casks secreted in Old Hunstanton and Thornham villages, and conveyed them safely to his Excise Office. A substantial quantity remained at large until Turner, supported only by Christopher Stangroom[1], raided the premises of William Hutchinson, a known malefactor and smuggler with a history of violent behaviour, who lived in a small cottage adjacent to The Red House in Thornham. Whilst in the process of removing casks from an underground vault behind Hutchinson's cottage, Turner and Stangroom were surrounded, threatened and finally assaulted by Hutchinson and four of his associates, namely Thomas Lewis, Daniel Wilkinson, John Robbs and John Thorp. All five smugglers had been leading members of Franklyn's village army, and they demonstrated by their behaviour that they had lost none of their aggressive spirit, or indeed their old confrontational habits, since the downfall of their former employer. Within minutes, an armed mob of thirty supporters arrived directly from the Kings Head ale-house, in customary riotous mood. Further assaults on the Excise Officers were averted by the arrival on the scene of Samuel Rennett[2], the well respected Customs Riding Officer based in Thornham, and by the neighbouring farmer and merchant from the Red House, Henry Benton, both of whom exercised their local status in the community, and their powers of persuasion, to placate the mob.

It was not the end of the matter. In July the following year, late one Friday night, a troop of the 15th Light Dragoon Regiment rode into

[1] Christopher Stangroom, Excise Officer based at Snettisham, featured prominently in the activity leading to the Hunstanton murders two years later.
[2] Samuel Rennett also played a prominent role in the Hunstanton murders.

Thornham village and surrounded the cottages of Hutchinson, Lewis and Wilkinson. The three men were arrested, chained and taken to King's Lynn, where they were bundled into a post-chaise and conducted under escort to London. Once in the capital, they were committed to the notorious Newgate Prison, a primitive, disease-ridden hell-hole feared even by the most hardened criminals of an extremely violent era. The three men, speaking a strange, almost foreign-sounding Norfolk dialect, aroused first the curiosity, then the unwanted attention, of the criminal, mainly Cockney, inmates with whom they were forced to co-exist for a period of two months whilst awaiting their trials at the forthcoming Old Bailey Sessions. In truth, the lives of the three Norfolk men were threatened more seriously by their fellow prisoners than by the judge, prosecution and jury, when they eventually stood in the dock and were charged with riotous assembly, assaulting Excise Officers and rescuing seized smuggled goods. Even though the three smugglers were many miles distant from the protection of a local Norfolk jury, the prosecution was feeble, and the court proceedings, at times, laughable. The prosecution case depended largely upon the testimonies of Excise Officers Turner and Stangroom, and Customs Officer Rennett. The evidence given by these three men was treated with caution, because of their vested interest in gaining convictions, and because their status as Officers of Revenue was treated with even more suspicion within the metropolis than in the country at large. The only civilian witness to come forward was Henry Benton of the Red House, Thornham, who immediately reduced the seriousness of the proceedings to a farcical level by attempting to negotiate his travelling and accommodation expenses, for which he was reprimanded severely by the Judge. While Benton had one eye on the profit he might make from his time and trouble in attending the Old Bailey Sessions, the other eye was focussed firmly upon his future physical safety and security. Understandably, he was anxious to avoid alienating the smuggling community in whose midst he lived and worked back in his Norfolk village. He must have felt severely intimidated by the prospect of being instrumental in sending three of his neighbours to the gallows at Tyburn. Consequently, his testimony was confusing and vague, much to the irritation of the prosecution, who needed his witness to be specific in confirming the details necessary for obtaining convictions.

151

The Judge, Mr Baron Eyre, directed the jury to favour giving the benefit of the doubt to the three Defendants, and within minutes Hutchinson, Lewis and Wilkinson were found not guilty of all charges. The three men were released, but not before the Judge issued a stern warning. 'I cannot help supposing, he concluded, 'that you are men deeply engaged in this very dangerous practice of smuggling; it has brought you within an ace of capital punishment, and the Law has been administered with great mercy to you. Pray let this be a warning to you, to get your bread honestly, for if you do not, sooner or later that punishment will fall upon you'.

Inevitably, the warning fell upon deaf ears. The three Norfolk men returned to their village, to pursue their violent, dangerous and above all profitable life-style.

CAPTAIN JOSIAS ROGERS AND THE NORFOLK COAST
1783-1787

The end of the War of American Independence in 1783 enabled the British Government to employ a much greater proportion of its regular armed forces in the domestic war against smuggling. We have seen in previous chapters how army regiments returning from action abroad helped to control the escalating supremacy of smuggling gangs on land. At sea, the situation was similar. Naval Captains returned in their warships from America in great numbers, and at the beginning of the year 1784 the Admiralty was able to deploy much of its fleet on smuggling duty around the entire British coastline. Four heavily-armed ships were assigned to the North Sea, and operated out of the ports of Great Yarmouth, King's Lynn, Boston and Hull; the *Myrmidon*, with 20 guns and a crew of 140 men, was the largest of these warships, and was supported by three 14-gun brig-sloops named the *Speedy*, the *Brazen* and the *Otter*.

Throughout the year 1784, pressure from the authorities against well-established smuggling gangs was almost relentless, in the maritime villages of England as a whole, and of Norfolk in particular. Inevitably, the smuggling barons, determined to preserve their ascendancy, retaliated by increasing the ferocity of their behaviour; the murders at Old Hunstanton in that year were by no means exceptional. As both sides strove without compromise for supremacy, the arrival of the Royal Navy, in the North Sea, the English Channel and the Irish Sea, was a decisive factor in a desperate attempt to quell the smuggling epidemic.

Captain Josias Rogers was the spear-head of the Admiralty's invasion of the coastal waters of the troublesome Norfolk region. Typical of the naval commanders of his day, he was courageous but reckless, a leader who administered discipline aboard ship to the point of cruelty, and who valued financial gain from plundering enemy ships with an avarice which was obsessive. The pursuit of prize-money rather than patriotic duty in the War against the American colonists led Captain Rogers to heroic, but injudicious engagements which resulted in the loss of two Admiralty ships to the enemy, two extremely harsh spells of imprisonment in enemy hands, and severe personal physical injury. He suffered the indignity of facing a court martial on two occasions, firstly for the loss during his command of H.M. Sloop *Harlem*, and later for the loss of H.M. Sloop *General Monk*, in 1779 and 1782 respectively. Although he was acquitted by the Lords of the Admiralty on both occasions, on account of his leadership qualities during the course of the War in America, he was nevertheless forced to return to England in temporary disgrace on a merchant vessel, and disembarked in London in September 1782.

After almost a year ashore, on half pay, Rogers was recalled to full-time duty, in August 1783, as commander of a newly-constructed, 14-gun Admiralty brig-sloop the *Speedy*, and in January 1784, he anchored at Yarmouth to prepare for action on the North Sea. His brief was to patrol the coastline of Suffolk, Norfolk and Lincolnshire, as far north as the Humber Estuary, to intercept pirate vessels, which frequently terrorised coastal villages, to protect the Yarmouth herring fleet, and above all to wage war on the smuggling trade.

His first taste of action in domestic waters involved testing the capability of the four-pounder guns aboard the *Speedy* against a fleet of Dutch sloops five leagues off Winterton. For some years previously, Dutch vessels had wreaked havoc upon the Yarmouth fishing industry by sabotaging nets and plundering catches. For Captain Rogers, the minor and one-sided skirmish against the Dutch proved no more that a muscle-flexing exercise; uppermost in his mind was the plunder and prize-money to be gained from overpowering smuggling vessels heavily laden with contraband.

Initially, his acquisitive instinct was frustrated by the versatility of purpose-built smuggling vessels, whose shallow draught allowed potential prey 'to slip through my fingers, as I was not able to follow over the shoals and sand-banks which infest this coast'[1]. However, he was soon rewarded for his persistence. On 21st February 1784, whilst cruising off Happisburgh, he observed 'a very fine cutter, with carriage guns mounted', which he presumed correctly to be a smuggling vessel. He gave chase and finally captured the *Nancy* from Ostend, captained by a well-known smuggler from Bacton by the name of Charles Gee[2]. On board was a treasure trove of contraband, in excess of one thousand gallons of brandy, rum and Geneva, over three tons of tea, and many other valuable commodities. Captain Rogers escorted the *Nancy* into Yarmouth harbour, complete with smugglers and some of the cargo. From this single seizure, the Captain would gain considerable financial reward from the eventual sale of the goods by auction at the Yarmouth Customs House, especially as he was solely responsible for the cutter's capture, and would not have to share his portion of the prize money with other officers. Nevertheless, Rogers could not resist the temptation to retain aboard the *Speedy* a significant quantity of the seized goods, either for his own personal use, or to sell directly to any number of willing purchasers on land, without parting with a percentage of the proceeds to the auction house or the Customs Board.

[1] Like all naval commanders, Captain Rogers kept a log aboard ship and recorded in detail day to day events.

[2] Charles Gee was one of many Norfolk smugglers who lived in Northern France and Belgium and who used his local Norfolk contacts to run quantities of contraband ashore. His favoured landing beaches were in the Cromer area. In August 1784, his laden vessel was pursued by the Yarmouth-based *Hunter* Customs Cutter, commanded by Captain Fisher. Both vessels became becalmed off Salthouse beach. Captain Fisher lowered his ten-oared long boat, and sent his 2nd Mate, Robert Jay and ten mariners, with instructions to board the smuggling lugger. Charles Gee's response to the attempt to board his vessel was to discharge a blunderbuss at the 2nd Mate, instantly killing him. Warrants for the arrest of Charles Gee for murder were subsequently issued, but he was never detained or brought to trial. Robert Jay was buried in Bacton churchyard, where his gravestone stands to this day. Such was the fear of Charles Gee and his gang in the area, that the gravestone merely records that Robert Jay was 'accidentally killed'.

The following morning, while the enormous seizure was being transferred from the decks of the *Nancy* to the Customs House, an Officer of Customs, Mr Place, acting upon information received, boarded Captain Rogers' brig-sloop. Exercising his considerable powers of search, he ordered the Captain to unlock the doors to the rear of the ship's bread room. Mr Place was not surprised to find secreted 36 gallons of Geneva, 18 gallons of brandy, 11 gallons of cordial water, 200 pounds of tea, 19 pounds of coffee, and a quantity of tobacco. The matter was subsequently reported to Customs headquarters in London, who in turn directed the Yarmouth Customs Collector to charge the acquisitive Captain with wrongful and substantial withholding of a large part of his seizure. Rogers was granted the opportunity to answer the charges against him, and he duly proffered a number of unconvincing excuses for his conduct. In one letter to the Customs Board, he explained that

'the *Nancy* cutter was the first seizure I have made since returning from the War against the American colonists. During that War, I was present at the capture of many enemy vessels, and whenever anything was found on board that would either nourish or encourage my crew, a part was retained for that purpose'.

He claimed to have assumed that such practice, of withholding some of the seizure *'in order to give my crewmen something to comfort them after being exposed to great hardship in the longboats all night, in quest of smugglers'*, would be acceptable in home waters. In another letter to the Customs Board, he explained that it had been his intention to deliver to the Customs House the illegally retained goods *'after he realised, to his surprise, that the quantity exceeded by far the needs of his crew; unfortunately, the Customs Officer had boarded the Speedy and discovered the goods before the opportunity presented itself'*.

Captain Rogers' lame representations were accepted with reluctance by the Customs board, but not before the Admiralty had intervened on behalf of its errant employee. He escaped with a severe censure and was allowed to retain the prize-money for the entire contents of the *Nancy*, a sum in excess of one year's Admiralty salary. In addition, he requested, and was granted, the right to employ the seized smuggling cutter as a tender vessel to the *Speedy*. This was of strategic importance to Rogers. The *Nancy* was a superb cutter of 58 tons burthen, and had been built in Dover for the specific purpose of smuggling off the Norfolk coast. She had an extremely shallow draft of only eight feet of water, and would be ideal for pursuit over the local shoals and sandbanks of which he had recently complained. Rogers renamed his new acquisition the *Lady Hammond* and promptly appointed his younger brother Thomas, a midshipman aboard the *Speedy*, as her commander. After two court-martials, and allegations relating to the retention of smuggled goods, a touch of nepotism seemed almost inconsequential.

Fortified with two perfectly equipped and armed sailing vessels, Captain Rogers was able to carry the fight to the smugglers in the North Sea with a vengeance, for a further two and a half years. As part of the continuing offensive against the coast and villages of north-west Norfolk, the Admiralty instructed its Captain to concentrate his efforts upon that troubled region. A number of heavily laden smuggling cutters were apprehended in the ensuing months with little difficulty, in view of the superior sea-going strength at his disposal, and it was not until June 1784 that he encountered opposition that was determined to dispute his temporary supremacy. In the early evening of 10th June, the *Speedy* was cruising two leagues off Holkham; the crew were engaged in general cleaning and maintenance duties. At 9 pm, a large lugger, which Rogers knew to be a smuggling vessel, came into view and was seen heading for the shore. Rogers manned and armed two longboats and sent them in chase of the lugger, with the object of boarding her. The response from the lugger was a bombardment of several broadsides of cannon, fired as a warning, causing the pursuing long-boats to back off and return to the *Speedy*. Two days later, Rogers observed the same lugger at anchor in Thornham Creek. Again, he manned and armed his longboats, and sent a boarding party under the command of his Lieutenant into the Old Harbour Channel, a highly dangerous manoeuvre in view of the violent reputation of the smuggling community which, as we have seen, infested this particular village. The smugglers' response was predictable. A heavy bombardment, fired from the New Harbour Channel[1], across an expanse

---

1 From 1700 to the end of the 18th century, there were in use two navigable harbours in Thornham, each served by its own harbour channel. The Old Harbour Channel, to the east, was the original medieval maritime approach to the village, and the medieval harbour was in all likelihood situated in the Oldfield Green area. The New Harbour Channel, to the West, came into regular use at the beginning of the 18th century, and gave access to the harbour used to this day. It was in the creek leading to this harbour that the smuggling vessel was at anchor.

of marsh, forced the Lieutenant to retreat once again, and to return to the *Speedy* with some casualties amongst his crew. Captain Rogers, observing from the decks of his brig sloop yet another humiliation, was outraged. 'The next morning', he wrote to the Admiralty, 'I determined to land with an even greater party of crew, in order to punish so great an insult'. With his newly-acquired knowledge of the complex system of creeks leading to his quarry, he launched three longboats, once again fully manned and armed, but on this occasion under his own personal command, into the New Harbour Channel. The numerical odds were not in his favour, as he found at the harbour's edge a hostile gathering of 'forty or more smugglers, armed, with a flag of defiance hoisted on the shore, threatening with the severest imprecations to murder my entire crew, should we not desist from attempting to seize their vessel'. Undaunted, Rogers' longboats pulled ever closer to the harbour. The intimidating sight of the approaching flotilla, with all three boats proudly displaying a Royal Navy ensign, and with the entire crew wielding cutlasses and brandishing fire-arms, revived painful memories in the minds of village smugglers, many of whom carried physical scars inflicted during the last major skirmish with government forces, on New Year's Eve 1782, just eighteen months previously. Their verbal bravado dissipated, and panic ensued. Fearing that their prized lugger, believed locally to be the fastest sail on the coast, and measuring 80 feet in length, would be seized and impounded by the approaching naval force, the villagers deliberately scuttled the vessel, allowing it to fill rapidly with water, thereby temporarily grounding it. Captain Rogers, meanwhile, advanced towards the harbour-side landing jetties, sent his men ashore, and after a brief engagement put to flight the dispirited opposition. At the same time, he seized a small cutter, containing a quantity of contraband, at anchor in the creek. To complete a most successful operation, he experienced the great satisfaction of seeing the smugglers' scuttled lugger, having grounded itself on a sandbank with deep water fore and aft, break up into two parts as the tide receded. The vessel was totally destroyed, beyond repair.

An independent observer, who wrote an eye witness account of the incident in the *Norfolk Chronicle*, suggested that Captain Rogers was being modest about his victory over the Thornham smugglers in the New Harbour. The observer calculated that Rogers' force of thirty men was confronted by a village mob consisting of over one hundred determined and aggressive individuals, considerably in excess of the forty opponents mentioned in the Captain's report to the Admiralty. Equally modest was Rogers' claim to his employers that, after dispersing the smugglers, he was able to seize 150 casks of spirits from the small cutter anchored in the creek. According to the observer ashore, Rogers' seizure consisted of more than '500 tubs of foreign spirits and a quantity of tea'. Evidently, the acquisitive Captain was up to his old tricks, retaining for his own use and disposal an even greater proportion of this latest seizure than on the occasion which caused him to be severely censured. Regardless of how many gallons of spirits were seized, it is evident that an unspecified quantity reached neither the security hold of the *Speedy*, nor the cellars of the King's Lynn Customs House. An entry in the Captain's log, for the day following the seizure in Thornham creek, suggests strongly a degree of on-board pilfering, by recording that 'whilst anchored in 5 fathoms of water off Thornham, I instructed my bosun to punish one Thomas Morris, crew-man, with 12 lashes for drunkenness'.

Following the decisive action in Thornham harbour creek, the name and reputation of Captain Rogers became greatly feared by maritime and land-based smugglers, along the entire length of Norfolk coastline, and his authority was never again seriously challenged in that region. He continued to harass the smuggling communities and their vessels in North Norfolk for the remainder of 1784, the whole of 1785 and 1786, in which year, as we have seen in an earlier chapter, he devoted much of his energy and maritime expertise to pursuing and apprehending William Kemball, when the infamous smuggler resumed his career following his acquittal. Captain Rogers was rewarded for his North Sea and Norfolk coast exploits, not only by financial gain from his seizures, whether legitimate or otherwise, but by promotion granted by his employers. Clearly impressed by his qualities of courage and leadership, the Admiralty advanced him, in late 1787, to post rank, to command warships carrying in excess of 20 guns, a promotion which took the Captain away from smuggling duties in the North Sea. At the same time, he married and purchased an estate in Boldre, Hampshire, from the proceeds of his successful exploits on the Norfolk coast. The French Revolution in 1789, followed by the Napoleonic Wars, brought Captain Rogers once more into direct conflict with enemy fleets. He served with great distinction and success in the West Indies, harassing French vessels in the West Indies, and took part in naval operations against the

French-held Islands of Martinique and Guadeloupe, and the recapture of the Island of Grenada.

Captain Rogers' energies and ambitions came to a sad and premature end at the age of forty, when he contracted yellow fever, and died on board his last ship, HMS *Quebec*. He was buried on the Island of Grenada, alongside the bodies of his younger brother Lieutenant James Rogers and his nephew Midshipman Josias Rogers, who both contracted the same fatal disease.

APPENDIX A

List of Jurors empanelled to serve at the Thetford Assizes, March 1785.

Name	Parish of Residence
Francis Blomfield	Swaffham
Benjamin Frost	Shingham
George Leech	Foulden
Thomas Stockings	Hilborough
Thomas Collison	Beachamwell
Francis Barsham	Wimbotsham
Thomas Lister	Upwell
Joseph Cole	Upwell
Christopher Thorpe	Stow Bardolph
Thomas Rowe	Outwell
Roger Jay	Ashill
Keene Bunhall	Thompson
Edward Clarke	Saham Toney
Robert Brookes	Carbrooke
John Boyce	Roudham
Anthony Porter	Great Ellingham
James Bernard the younger	Great Ellingham
John Turner	Great Ellingham
Thomas Steward	Great Ellingham
William Hardy	Rockland All Saints
Samuel Cubit	Attleborough
Robert Payne	Attleborough
William Chapman	Attleborough
John Foulsham	Attleborough
Ezekiel Read	Bridgham
John Nurse	Hockham
William Griffin	Mundford
Francis King	Northwold
John Gooch	North Lopham
Thomas Syder	Banham
John Jolly	Banham
John Rush	Banham
John Palmer	Rushford with Snare Hill
James Turner	Blo Norton
James Murton	Blo Norton
Lionel Rodwell	East Harling

APPENDIX B

List of Customs, Excise and Army mounted officers and men assembled in Old Hunstanton on the night of 25th/26th September 1784.

Customs Officers.

Thomas Mitchell, from Wells
William Green, from Snettisham
Samuel Rennett, from Thornham
Abel Dawson, from Brancaster

Excise Officers

Christopher Stangroom, from Snettisham
Francis Young, from Snettisham
Thomas Jarvis, from Kings Lynn

15th Regiment of Light Dragoons

Lieutenant Polhill, billeted at Kings Lynn
Lieutenant Wheelock, billeted at Wells
Private Jardine, billeted at Wells
Private Powell, billeted at Wells
Private Stevens, billeted at Wells
Sergeant Major Leishman, billeted at Wells
Private Mantle, billeted at Wells
Private Kitchen, billeted at Wells
Private Moulder, billeted at Wells
Sergeant Paine, billeted at Snettisham
Corporal Holmes, billeted at Snettisham
Private Matthews, billeted at Snettisham
Private Goff, billeted at Snettisham
Private Melvin, billeted at Snettisham
Corporal Stevenson, billeted at Burnham Mkt.
Private Gristwood, billeted at Burnham Mkt.
Private Webb, billeted at Burnham Mkt.

PRIMARY SOURCES

Public Record Office, Kew

Boards of Customs and Excise: CUST 18, 37, 41, 48, 51, 96, 97,
The Admiralty: ADM 1, 7, 12, 51,
The War Office: WO 1, 2, 3, 4, 5, 12, 17, 27, 34
The Home Office: HO 43, 47,
The Privy Council: PC1
The Treasury: T1, 2, 11, 27, 29, 44, 48, 64
The Assizes: ASSI 25, 33, 34, 35,
The Exchequer: E 125, 126, 127, 128, 129, 130, 134, 159, 165, 176, 218,
The Kings Bench: KB1

The Guildhall Library, London

Old Bailey Sessions Papers

Norfolk Record Office, Norwich

Documents in the classes of The Quarter Sessions, Petty Sessions, miscellaneous smuggling cases, and Parish Registers.

Norwich Local History Library

The Norfolk Chronicle, 1783 to 1787
The Norwich Mercury, 1783 to 1787

Documents privately held by Mr Terry Greenacre

Depositions relating to the Trials of Kemball, Gunton and Franklyn
Transcripts of the Trials of Kemball and Gunton

INDEX

For the benefit of parish and family historians, all names and places have been indexed except for those in the appendices.The following abbreviations have been used: Burnham Mkt. for Burnham Market, Dere. for Dereham, Fak. for Fakenham, K. Lynn for King's Lynn, Old Hunst. for Old Hunstanton, Snett. for Snettisham, Thet. for Thetford. Entries printed in *italics* are newspapers; entries printed in ***bold italics*** are ships.

Eaton, 63
Ellis, John, 78
Ellison, Cornet Henry, 18
Elmham, North, 52
Emneth, 64, 68
Exchequer, 8, 60, 86, 87, 92, 93, 148
Excise, Board of, 4, 14, 93, 97, 98, 148, 149
Excise Officers, 9, 14, 16, 26, 28, 33, 59, 65, 79, 98, 99, 103, 113, 116, 122, 123, 127, 134, 147, 148, 150, 151 See also Bliss, Robert
Experiment, 39

Fairy, 91, 93
Fakenham, 103
Fall, Daniel, 74
Fearnought, 73
Felmingham, 67
Ferret, John, 64
Fettlebridge Common, 65
Flint, John, 64, 68, 79
Flushing, Netherlands, 4, 108
Forshaw, family, 125; Robert, 89
Forster, Elizabeth, 67
Foulden, 69
Foulsham, 78,
Franklyn, John, 105
Franklyn, Thomas, 4, 65, 97, 99-117, 121, 127, 128, 131, 134, 135, 138, 140, 144-148, 150
Frost, Benjamin, 69
Frostwick, Daniel, 55, 73

Gabbett, Lieut. Colonel, 141, 144, 145, 146
Garner, John, 64, 69, 84, 86
Gaywood, 51, 52, 135
Gee, Charles, 57, 154
General Monk, 153

Gibson, Thomas, 115
Gooch, James, 60, 76, 77, 78
Gray, Captain William, 18, 61, 63, 145
Green, William, 1, 32, 33, 45-48, 51, 55, 56, 66, 69, 70, 71, 72, 73, 79, 86, 89, 102, 117, 124, 125, 127, 156; Phoebe, 48, 55, 86
Greenacre, Martin, 95
Greyhound, 37, 168
Gristwood, Pte. Thomas, 24
Gt Ellingham, 69
Gt Hockham, 70
Guildhall, 2, 3, 67, 115, 140, 146, 147
Gunton, Andrew, 1, 6, 43, 46, 49, 50, 51, 52, 53, 55, 57, 59, 60, 61, 62, 63, 64, 65, 67, 70-79, 80, 82, 86, 87, 92, 148

Hall, John, 68
Haman, Robert, 68
Happisburgh, 5, 12, 154
Hardy, William, 60, 77
Harlem, 153
Hays, Thomas, 138, 140, 141
Heacham, 29, 49, 50, 111, 114, 116, 132, 147, 150
Hethersett, 63
Hilborough, 69
Hockering, 84
Holkham, 123, 156
Holman, Mary, 105
Holme, 4, 29, 32, 88, 100, 104, 105, 109, 111, 114, 132, 147, 149, 150
Holt, 28, 100, 103
Hoste, Rev. Dixon, 24, 49, 50, 53
Houghton, James, 55
Houghton Hall, 75
Huggins, Thomas, 115
Hull, Yorks., 39, 91, 152

North Lopham, 60, 78
North Tuddenham, 84
North Walsham, 28, 63, 67
Northwold, 78
Norwich, 9, 26, 28, 50, 51, 52, 53,
    59, 60, 61, 62, 63, 64, 68, 70,
    73, 80, 81, 84, 85, 86, 87, 95,
    99, 101, 102, 113, 134, 146,
    147, 148
Norwich Mercury, 26, 95, 99, 148
Nurse, James 70

Old Bailey, 58, 151
Otter, 41, 126, 152
Overton, William, 121, 124, 125,
    129

Paine, Sergeant Thomas, 11
Palmer, John, 78
Payne, Robert, 69
Peddars Way, 111, 112
Pitt Arms, 18, 24, 31, 103, 123
Place, Mr, 67, 155
Polhill, Lieut., 46, 50
Press gang, 6, 25, 40, 74, 92, 134,
    138-141, 146
Prison hulks, 53, 54, 70

Quarter Sessions, 5, 27, 115, 135,
    148
Quebec, 159

Rand, Thomas, 46, 129
Randall, Robert, 63, 68, 84
Read, Ezekiel, 70
Rennett, Samuel, 32, 33, 42, 45,
    46, 48, 49, 150, 151
Renuck, Peter Jacques, 73
Repulse, 39
Revenge, 89, 91
Riding Officers, 12, 13, 14, 32, 57,
    104

Ringstead, 31, 32, 33, 42, 55, 73,
    103, 104, 111, 112
Rishton, Martin ffolkes, 146
Robbs, John, 150
Roberts, Henry, 78; William, 78
Rockland All Saints, 60
Rodney, 88
Rogers, Lieut. James, 159;
    Midshipman Josias, 159; Capt.
    Josias, 89, 91, 93, 152-159
Rushford, 78, 160

Sandringham, 51
Sayer, Robert, 120
Seaman, Peter, 70
Sedgeford, 33
Sheering, John, 78
Shelbourne, Lord, 149
Sheldrake, Martin, 55
Sheriff of Norfolk, 60, 62, 63, 80,
    131, 133, 135
Sheringham, 12, 28
Shouldham, 69
Slater, William, 115
Smith, Perry, 9, 36, 43, 46
Smyth, James, 55; John, 73, 74
Snettisham, 1, 10, 11, 16, 28, 32,
    33, 45, 48, 49, 50, 52, 69, 79,
    86, 150
Southgate, William, 121, 125, 126,
    127, 128, 129
Sparham, 52
Sparshall, Thomas, 64, 68
Speedy, 5, 41, 89, 92, 152, 153,
    154, 155, 156, 158
Spencer, William, 99, 100, 122,
    131, 146, 147
Stanfield, 52
Stangroom, Christopher, 10, 11,
    16, 32, 33, 36, 42, 45, 47, 50,
    71, 72, 74, 79, 92, 150, 151
Stanhoe, 64, 68, 84

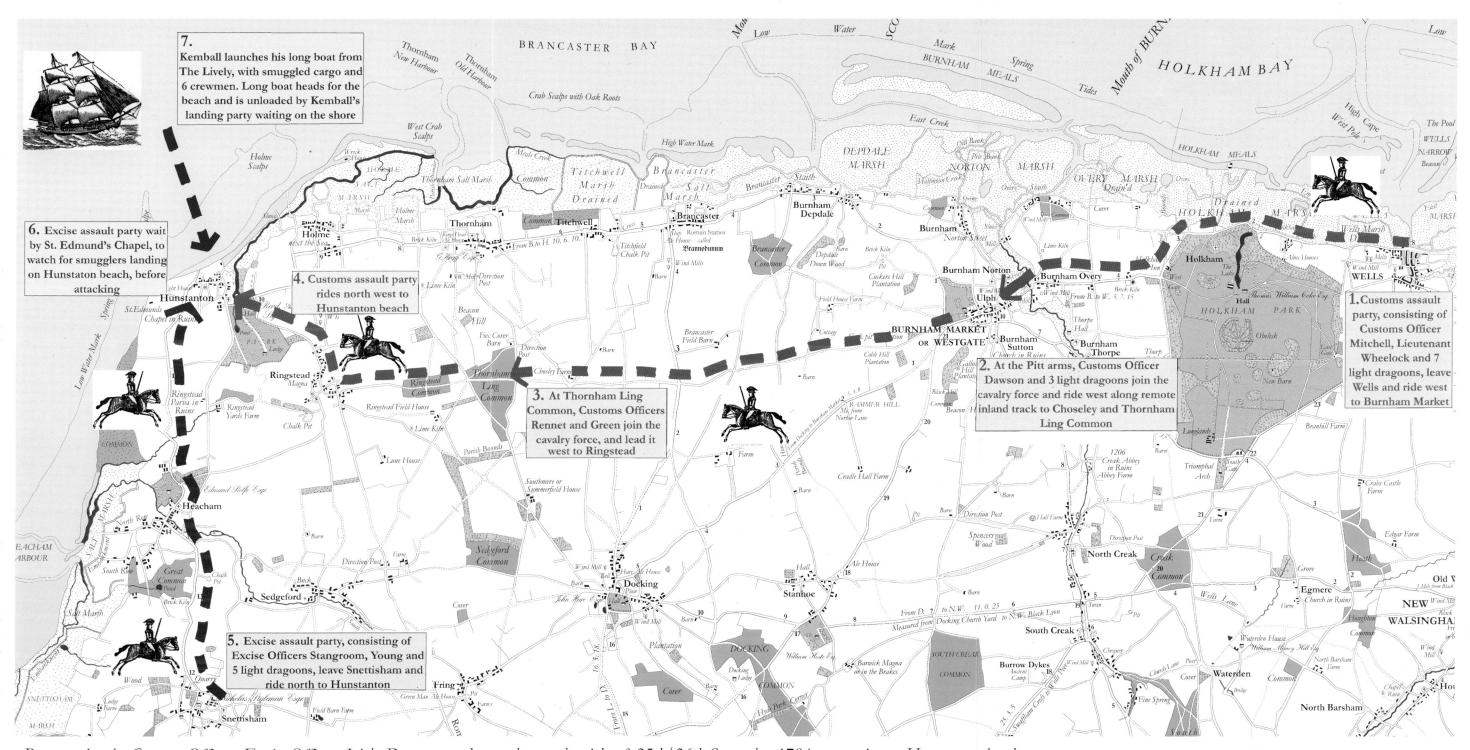

7. Kemball launches his long boat from The Lively, with smuggled cargo and 6 crewmen. Long boat heads for the beach and is unloaded by Kemball's landing party waiting on the shore

6. Excise assault party wait by St. Edmund's Chapel, to watch for smugglers landing on Hunstanton beach, before attacking

4. Customs assault party rides north west to Hunstanton beach

3. At Thornham Ling Common, Customs Officers Rennet and Green join the cavalry force, and lead it west to Ringstead

5. Excise assault party, consisting of Excise Officers Stangroom, Young and 5 light dragoons, leave Snettisham and ride north to Hunstanton

2. At the Pitt arms, Customs Officer Dawson and 3 light dragoons join the cavalry force and ride west along remote inland track to Choseley and Thornham Ling Common

1. Customs assault party, consisting of Customs Officer Mitchell, Lieutenant Wheelock and 7 light dragoons, leave Wells and ride west to Burnham Market

Routes taken by Customs Officers, Excise Officers, Light Dragoons and smugglers on the night of 25th/26th September 1784, converging on Hunstanton beach. taken from Andrew Macnair's digital redrawing of Faden's 1797 Map of Norfolk www.fadensmapofnorfolk.co.uk